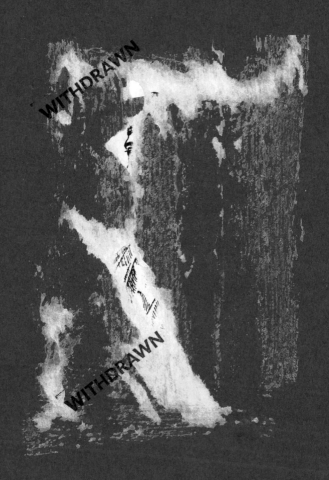

# Don Potter:
# an inspiring century

Vivienne Light

Canterton Books

# Don Potter:
# an inspiring century

ISBN        0-9541627-1-4

Published by    Canterton Books
                Forest Ford
                Brook
                Hampshire
                SO43 7HF
                UK

                www.cantertonbooks.com2.info

Printed by      Brown & Son
                Crow Arch Lane
                Ringwood
                Hampshire
                BH24 1PD
                UK

Book Design     Sarah Jane Jackson
                Type-set in Gill Sans Light and Perpetua

First Published September 2002

# Contents

Don Potter

Don Potter is a remarkable man.

Above all he is a great teacher as many generations of Bryanston students can confirm. His enthusiasm and the twinkle in his eye are quite magnetic and he has caused many an uninterested student to become motivated and lit the flame of creativity in many a damp, dull soul.

I was at Bryanston during the war years when life was exceedingly austere. We were all hungry and cold but Don brought a cheerful energy into our lives in the metalwork, sculpture and particularly the pottery departments. He took our minds off Latin prep and the war by getting us to think and make creatively - you just longed to finish your tedious school work so you could get back to one of Don's departments. They didn't seem like school, they seemed like a hobby and very quickly they became a hobby.

My best memories are of the below stairs pottery with its wood fired kiln which reached terrific temperatures because of the hugely tall Bryanston chimneys. I remember the all night firings, keeping the kiln stoked with wood and waiting for the cones to melt to indicate that it had reached the right temperature for our galena or wood ash glazes.

I am sure we shouldn't have been allowed to stay up all night and certainly we shouldn't have been drinking beer or cider but we would then have missed Don talking about his time with Eric Gill, wearing kilts whilst carving the outside of BBC in Portland Place, his enthusiasm for slipware and Thomas Toft, stories about St Ives and Bernard Leach's pottery and his admiration for the work of Michael Cardew.

He talked and inspired us throughout the day and night and showed us how

# Foreword
Terence Conran

i

to make things with consummate ease. I certainly would not have been able to achieve the things that I have in my life if he had not taught me the practical skills of welding and forging, potting and casting, sculpting and carving. But most of all, he imbued us all with the pleasure of making things. He showed us the glow you can get from seeing an idea turn into a three dimensional, beautiful object.

He gets enormous pleasure from his own work, particularly his sculpture and beautiful carved lettering. I saw him just after his 100th birthday chipping away at a huge piece of heavy oak, which he proceeded to lift to show how strong he still is. Although I'm thirty years younger, I could only just move it!

He is and always has been a tower of strength in every way. Thank you Don, you have been a great inspiration to many people and helped them make their lives much more creative and interesting.

12 July, 2002

The existence of this book, *Don Potter: an inspiring century,* is due in good part to the sculptor, Mary Spencer Watson. I had been to see Mary in order to talk about her own work in the course of gathering material for a Dorset book which was to be a sequel to *Re-inventing the landscape: contemporary painters and Dorset.* During our conversation she said: 'You really ought to go and see Don Potter at Bryanston…a marvellous man'. She gave me his telephone number, I rang and spoke to Mary Potter, Don's wife, who said 'Yes, do come', and the rest, as they say, is history. Having spent many hours with both Don and Mary, I decided to put the 'second Dorset book' on hold and to write a book dedicated to the life and work of this extraordinary and charismatic man.

Such a task would have been impossible without the support and patience of Don and Mary, their children Anne and Julian, and a close friend of the Potters and Bryanston School Archivist, Alan Shrimpton. Without the excellent support of Sarah Jane Jackson in designing the book, and Isobel Colbourn's editorial work on the manuscript, this book would not have had any chance of meeting its deadline, which was to publish in time for Don's Retrospective Exhibition at Dorset County Museum, Dorchester, which also marks his hundredth year.

Many, many people have given me information and help for which I am truly grateful; their names and further acknowledgements appear later in the book. A special thank you must go to Sir Terence Conran for his Foreword, which I believe catches the mood of the book, and for his support in this venture. A further special thank you must go to my husband, Paul, for his encouragement and to Hilary, our youngest daughter, for her help and forbearance!

Don has been many things in the course of his long life. In my research I have discovered that this was a man greatly respected by the late Lord Baden-Powell during the early days of Scouting; a sculptor of such skill that Eric Gill assigned to him most of his wood carving commissions; an architectural stone sculptor of great talent; a rope-spinner entertainer; a musician; an excellent potter in the Studio Pottery tradition; an inspirational teacher who taught at

# Introduction
Vivienne Light

Bryanston School for over forty years; and a much valued friend to countless people. Many of his former pupils have themselves since achieved distinguished careers in the arts. Many others, although working in different spheres of life, have felt Don's formative influence on their lives in some special way. I have been able to weave many Bryanstonian memories into the text, but inevitably these are but a small sample.

To write about Don has not been the easiest of tasks. He has never kept a systematic record, or indeed <u>any</u> kind of record, of his work. However, responding to my initial request, Mary and Don gathered various folders and filled them with an assortment of newspaper cuttings, photographs and fragments of writing in Don's hand. Few dates and details were attached to any of this archive material, and as 'detective work' got under way it became apparent that some quite special carvings were missing from Don's photograph collection altogether. Although I have succeeded in identifying the whereabouts of a good number of Don's sculptures I am sure that the list is not comprehensive. Selecting illustrations for this book has involved some difficult choices; the aim has been to show as wide a spectrum of Don's work as possible.

The fact that Don has never been overtly concerned with keeping a record of what he has done is symptomatic of a man, who (in Dinah Batterham's words) is 'a doer'. It is also indicative of someone who has never felt a burning need to have his individuality as an artist recognised. He once wrote regarding sculpture : 'The cult of originality has become a sterilising obsession; only very few of us can become a Maillol, a Henry Moore, a Zadkine or a Picasso'. However, after leaving Eric Gill, Don did find his own voice, his own personal mode of expression, his own point of departure.

William Blake has always been a firm favourite with Don. Wingfield Digby (in the 1950s), once wrote of this poet: 'Blake never proselytised, crusaded, or sought to found a school or movement. He was superbly creative, like a prodigy of nature. What he made of himself, his simple life and happiness was not the least of the achievements for which he is remembered' (see page 75). I believe that much the same could be said of Don. It has been a joy to record something of his life to date.

27 July, 2002

# Don Potter:
# an inspiring century

One has to wonder whether Donald Potter was born with the same luxurious mane of hair which he still possesses at a hundred years of age. Unfortunately, there is no sure means of knowing, but one suspects that it might have been so.

A brief history of Donald's genealogy reveals that his paternal grandparents were Henry Joseph Potter and Fanny Bracken. Fanny had ten children, of whom Donald's father (christened Henry Joseph Potter after his father) was the eighth child. Don's maternal grandparents were John Henry Wheeler Matthews and Mary Jane Deathe. They met and married on the Isle of Wight, after which they moved to Newington in Kent. Here, Henry Matthews was Headmaster of Church House School for thirty-eight years [1] They had three children, the youngest of whom was Bessie Matthews. Bessie married Henry Potter and they had three children. Donald Steele Potter was the eldest child and only son.

Donald (hereafter referred to more familiarly as Don) was born on 21st April 1902. His two sisters were Norah Mary (born 1904) and Dorothy (born 1906). Norah trained as a primary school teacher at Bishop Otter College, Chichester. She never married. Dorothy married William Scott Kennedy quite late in life. They had one son, Lawrence, a talented flautist, who sadly died in a car accident in France.

# First Years

# 1902-1920

[1] John Henry Wheeler Matthews (grandfather) outside Church House School, Newington.
His granddaughter, Norah, is sitting on her mother's lap.

As a child, Don's first home was in the small Kentish village of Newington, on the main road to Sittingbourne. His accounts of early life there are somewhat redolent of Wordsworth's *Prelude*. He was able to wander freely, felt 'at one with nature' and was 'left to his own devices'. He loved the countryside: 'I was never happier than when I was exploring the hills, woods and the creeks along the River Medway, sensitive to the mystery and magic of it all.'[1]

Norah, at the age of seventy-eight, wrote about their early school days:

> My childhood was lived in an age of class distinction. When we reached school age there was no question of us being educated with the lower class village children, although my grandfather had been their headmaster for all his teaching days. A private school was a foregone conclusion. This sounds snobbish, but it was the existing social pattern. Newington - now completely changed from its rural charm….was a small beautiful village of apple and cherry orchards, farms and hop gardens. Newington seemed to be enveloped in snow at cherry blossom time, and the orchards assumed a rosy pink blush, when the apple buds unfolded……..There were no paths - the road was bordered on each side by hedges and ditches. The ditches were overgrown with grass and hedgerow weeds and were damp and muddy. Tramps begged for crusts at our door and gypsies brought round paper windmills and artificial flowers.
>
> In the village there were a few shops.. the sweetshop [was one]. We had a penny every Saturday and a packet of sweets could be bought for a farthing. There was a grocer's, a draper's, a butcher's, a post office and an Inn. About a mile down the road was the only school run by my grandfather, who was People's Warden at the Church, beloved by the village and ready with help for all who needed it. A brass plaque to his memory was placed in the North wall of the Church.
>
> We all started at the Convent of the Nativity when we were five years old. When Donald grew older he was allowed to ride his bike with Rose [daily maid] walking by the side. Often he would scare the wits out of poor Rose's head by riding down [Keycol] Hill with his feet on the handlebars! Each day we would [go] three miles to Sittingbourne carrying our mid-day sandwiches. Each evening we would [return]…..in those days people did walk.

From his earliest years Don loved to draw, and even as a child of eight he had an inherent feeling and talent for carving and handling sculptural materials. He would dig local clay from a site just five minutes away from his home, or work with modelling clay given to him by his parents to model figures. He would also carve lumps of chalk with a penknife and make walking sticks from hazel twigs.

One exceptional event he remembers from this time was seeing one of the first aeroplanes to fly the Channel. It landed in a field two miles away and his mother took him to see the plane. Crowds of people from around the country came and it was eventually covered with thousands of signatures. Don remembers:

> I came home fired by enthusiasm and set to work making a pair of cardboard wings which were fixed to my arms. The kitchen tablecloth was fixed to my wrists and ankles. Having climbed onto the top of our chicken house I took a leap into space and the next thing I knew was our neighbour helping me down the garden path in a very dilapidated condition![2]

This idyllic (if somewhat adventurous) life came to an end when his father's business 'Invicta Poultry, Dog and Game Food' [2] failed. The family had to sell their house and move to the town of Gillingham: 'a drab sprawl of a place with monotonous rows of houses'. Don was heartbroken. He contracted a mild form of TB which initially affected his wrists but had no long-term effect on his health.

[2] The Wheeler & Matthews business: Invicta Poultry, Dog and Game Food

Eventually, emotional release came for Don with two life-changing events, the significance of which did not emerge until some years later. One event was the use of a large open space behind his new home as a site for travelling circuses and fairs. He became fascinated by the fairground art, the 'decorative roundabouts', the 'elaborately carved horses' and the animals. He loved seeing the 'huge circus tents being put up and all the hustle and bustle that went with it'. There were also travelling Wild West Shows and he was spellbound by the skilful lassoing and rope-spinning that used to be part of such performances.

The second event, at about the age of twelve, was the discovery of a cello in a nearby junk shop. Christopher Wellington[3], Don's friend and former Bryanston pupil, has written that as a boy:

> Don listened attentively to the orchestra when he visited the cinema (silent cinema presented with instrumental accompaniment). The rich sound of the instrument particularly attracted him, so that when he saw the cello in the shop he immediately knew he must have it, although he did not have the necessary £2.10s to pay for it: it was a lot of money in those days. However the shop keeper allowed him to pay for it by instalments of five shillings a week.

He still remembers the moment when the cello was 'fetched off' the wall and he had 'this lovely big fiddle' in his arms. Don proudly took the cello home and strung it, but when he tried to play it, it made a curious 'wobbling noise'. Eventually he discovered that it had no sound post. Once this was corrected he started having lessons. Retrospectively, he has described the tone of this cello as 'like an old saw'. He says that he does not remember much about his first cello teacher except that he was 'a bit of a rogue'.

By the time Don had reached his twenties he had embarked on lessons at the London Cello School - at first with Alison Dalrymple, whom he describes as 'a nice person and a good teacher'. Later, at the end of his time with Eric Gill, he studied with Herbert Walenn. Don remembers, in particular, taking part in recitals with fifty other cellists, all playing together. His first, rather poor, cello was upgraded. Later, when at Bryanston, he was able to 'own a real aristocrat, an Italian Grancino'.

As a school-child Don maintains he was 'unteachable' and learnt nothing. However, he did become friends with the English school-master, E.E. Reynolds, of whom in later life he came to call 'Josh' Reynolds. Don felt Reynolds was

[3] Don aged about 15 years

always a great help to him; not least in introducing him to the Scout Movement. In later years Reynolds wrote *Sir Thomas More* (Burns Oates, London, 1953). He sent a copy to Don and inside the cover wrote as part of a dedication: 'Here is a copy of my Sir Thomas More. The reproductions of the Holbein pictures will at least interest you'.

Don was only twelve years old when the First World War broke out. He was at school for much of the war but left as soon as he could. He hated school and this is perhaps reflected in his last school report (1917). His final form position for the term's work and examination is given as 23rd out of 28, while his final position in the Mathematical Set as 28 out of 28! The Form Master's comment was:

> He is very good with any form of mechanical work, though he finds study difficult. He should however endeavour to better himself in spelling, writing, arithmetic and English - these are certainly essentials. He has in him the making of a fine, useful type of man.

The Headmaster wrote:

> Though he is by no means good at books, he should do very well in later life. His character is developing on the right lines. He is fitted for an out-of-doors life....[3].

For Don, however, leaving school and entering adult employment turned out to be somewhat akin to jumping out of the frying pan and into the fire. Don desperately wanted to be a craftsman but it was war-time and his father found him work at a munitions factory in the suburbs of North London. He worked from seven-thirty in the morning to six o'clock in the evening: 'it was awful; the nearest approach to prison I have ever known'. Altogether, he 'endured' work in three munitions factories:

> The first two were mass-production, but the last one turned out more specialised work connected with aircraft engines. I got a good dose of bullying and leg-pulling here, but I watched and talked to those men who seemed really skilled and learnt much of the craft of metalwork and the discipline that goes with it.

The skills which he acquired in metalwork were to later serve him well.

## Gilwell Park

Around 1915, the Potter family moved to Chingford in Essex. From here, over a period of three years, Don travelled to his hated work in three different munitions factories. However, Chingford was not far from Gilwell Park, a beautiful parkland estate on the borders of Epping Forest. In 1919, W. F. de Bois Maclaren[1] purchased the estate for ten thousand pounds and presented it as a gift to The Scout Association of Britain. Gilwell was to become the International Training Centre for Scoutmasters, and is now The Scout Association's Headquarters.

Don first joined the Scouts at Newington when he was about eight years old. The local Troop Leader was Josh Reynolds, his English Master at school [4]. There were already Boy's Brigades and cadet groups in existence, but when Don 'joined the Cadets for a short time [he] got so bored drilling and marching about and blowing bugles that he soon left'. He much preferred the Scouts where the 'momentum came from the boys'. What particularly appealed was the comradeship, the camping and hiking that went with Scouting.

# The Scouting Years: Gilwell Park, 1920 -1930

[4] Scout Camp.
Josh Reynolds ringed in the 3rd row back and Don, well brushed hair, standing to the right behind him.

Once the family was settled at Chingford, Don had the opportunity to re-join the Scouts. He joined a local troop at South Woodford, the Scout Master then being Rev. John Holyoak. The troop was frequently invited to visit Gilwell at weekends to help with various pioneering projects. Don remembers that 'the place was in quite a mess and very neglected, gates and fences needed mending, and the grounds were overrun by picnickers and the public'.

From his very first visit, Don fell in love with Gilwell and at the weekends he would escape from the munitions factory and camp in the grounds of the Park. As Byron Rogers wrote in a Sunday Telegraph Review (1996):[2]

> Here he became so fascinated by outdoor life he took it home with him, building himself a bed out of willow saplings which he was startled to find budded in spring, so that by summer he had disappeared into a bower of green leaves. Autumn, he said, was particularly beautiful in his bedroom.

A photograph was once taken of Don at the top of a tree at Gilwell [5]. It seems that not wanting to be beaten by two other Scouts, he climbed to the top of the tree way ahead of them, swung a lasso and then stood on his head. 'A bit of swanking' as Don now admits! His daughter, Anne,[3] has written:

> As a boy scout Don loved sleeping outside and said that he had roped himself into the top of a very tall spruce tree at Gilwell and slept the night there. When he used to visit us in the south of France in his 80's he always chose to sleep outside on the terrace where Jude my son often joined him.

In a small cottage to the right of the old entrance gates (now pulled down) lived Francis Gidney and his wife Marjory. Gidney, then affectionately known as 'Skipper Gidney' held the post of Camp Chief. Although he had been badly gassed during the war he maintained an infectious enthusiasm for life. Together with the founder of the Scout Movement, Baden-Powell (1857-1941), he ordered the affairs at Gilwell.

Over a number of evenings and weekends Don attended the Wood Badge course: the first Scoutmaster's training course ever held at Gilwell (1919). This advanced course involved, as it still does, new scout leaders acquiring a wide range of skills. The Wood Badge itself, which consists of two beads on a leather thong, was invented by Baden-Powell at the very time that Don and eighteen others successfully completed their training. Baden-Powell made these first

Wood Badges himself, using beads from a necklace originally belonging to Dinizulu, King of the Zulus. Baden-Powell had acquired this necklace during an African campaign in 1888. When the original beads were all used, replicas were made by Don, who continued carving Wood Badge beads until the day he left Gilwell.

From his earliest days, Don was actively encouraged in his wood-carving by Baden-Powell, who recognised in Don a talented sculptor with an instinctive feeling for wood. However, it was Gidney who bought Don his first set of wood-carving tools. With these, Don carved his first totem poles, walking sticks, trophies, emblems and shields. In the *Daily Mirror* of 10 September, 1924, there is a picture of Don taking part in a shield carving competition organised between different troops. The caption for the picture is 'The Happy Craftsman'!

One of Don's first major projects at Gilwell was to build a log camp-fire circle with a seventeen-foot totem pole. This totem ended in a carved buffalo skull. Following this carving, Don received further totem commissions from scout masters of other regions. On the back of one photograph [6] an inscription reads: 'Don's totem poles £10 each.' Each totem was finely carved, an art work unto itself [11].

By the age of twenty, Don had become a self-taught professional wood carver. Prospective purchasers from both within and beyond Gilwell were asking him to carry out specific wood-carving commissions. *The Jay* [7] was carved sometime in the 1920s. There are no details available as to who commissioned it.

[6] Totem poles, £10 each
[7] *Jay* Early wood-carving

# Don joins Gilwell Staff

In 1919 the munitions factory closed and at last Don was free. At this point Gidney invited him to become a permanent member of Gilwell's training staff; an invitation which Don accepted with alacrity. Don was now a King's Scout and a Patrol Leader for a new patrol called the Panther. Albert Beales was his 'Second', and they were assisted by Stanley Hall, just back from fighting in France.

Don found the mix of people who became scouts one of the most interesting factors about the organisation: 'people from all stations of life, farm-hands, school-masters, factory workers, Lords, Sirs and Peers of the Realm! At yearly reunions, all would pitch their tents along with Baden-Powell, who always slept in his Ashanti hammock.' In the evenings they would 'group round a great camp fire where B-P would make his speech.'[4]

Don, however, also recognised that on rare occasions The Scout Movement attracted people with a less wholesome motive. He recalls that once an incriminating diary belonging to an office worker was discovered while the latter was away at the Kunderstag Jamboree: 'He was met on his return at Waterloo Station with a note sacking him on the spot. He was so overcome that he was violently sick all over the shoes of the messenger who had brought the note!'[5]

# Friendship with Baden-Powell and totem carvings

Baden-Powell [8] was a constant visitor to Gilwell, which he felt was his show-piece: 'the heart of Scouting'. Don remembers him as 'a wonderful man, not at all pompous but relaxed and jovial, a gifted speaker with a terrific personality, friendly to all and very approachable'. Baden-Powell was a man with a distinguished military career who became a Major-General at the age of forty-three. It was his writing of *Aids to Scouting* which changed his life, and turned him from a soldier into a worker for peace.

One attribute of Baden-Powell's which Don greatly admired, was his artistic ability: his 'brilliant pen and ink sketches. He was ambidextrous and would draw and sketch with both hands.' Once he wrote an article for the Scout Magazine and illustrated it with a humorous cartoon of Don in his hiking gear. This was in response to Baden-Powell having observed a particular 'lone hiker' at his home, Pax Hill, in Bentley, Hampshire:

[8] Baden-Powell and Don at Gilwell
[9] Pax Hill, Bentley, Hampshire. Home of Lord Baden-Powell.

He had tramped it, carrying a long pack of his own making, slung like a ruck-sack on his back. This held his tent, bedding, cooking pots, etc. and he had a felling axe strapped to the side, as well as a long lariat. He carried with him a beautifully made bow, and arrows (in a very ornamental quiver) as well as a well carved staff.

His hunting knife had a handsome and comfortable handle of hickory, and its blade had been tempered by the Scout himself.[6]

Don camped at Baden-Powell's home several times [9]. It was from this address that the Chief Scout wrote to Don on a number of matters. One letter was to thank Don for a 'surprise' present of a carved crook stick [10]:

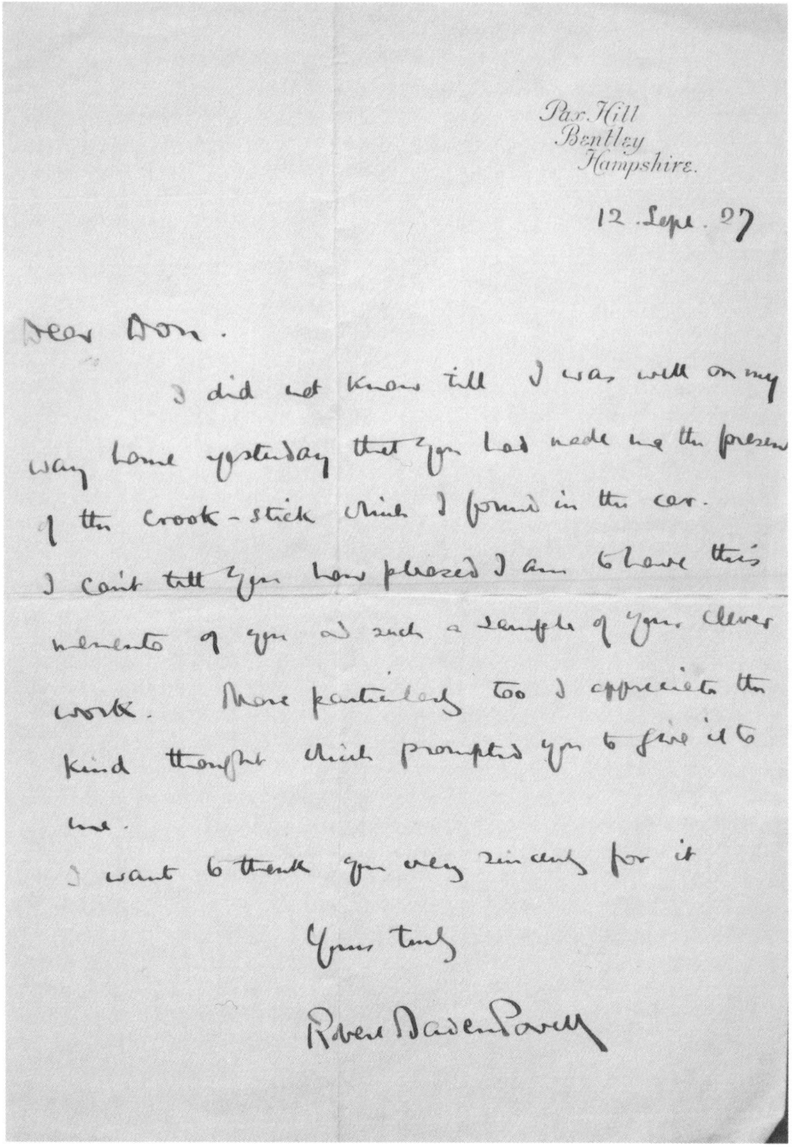

Par. Hill
Bentley
Hampshire.

12. Sept. 27

Dear Don.

I did not know till I was well on my way home yesterday that you had made me the present of the crook-stick which I found in the car. I can't tell you how pleased I am to have this memento of you as such a sample of your clever work. More particularly too I appreciate the kind thought which prompted you to give it to me.

I want to thank you very sincerely for it

Yours truly

Robert Baden-Powell

[10] Letter from Baden-Powell

In another letter (28 June 1928), Baden-Powell asked Don to send him a photograph of himself beside the 'graven image of the owl' which Don had carved for the 4th Cardiff Troop. The carving was to commemorate members who had died in the War.

Earlier in that same year (2 February, 1928) Baden-Powell had also written to ask whether Don could make use of:

> some limbs off the old yew trees here…… The trees are a 1000 years old (according to an authority from Kew) and it seems a pity to use them as firewood. I thought if they were carvable we might make some totems of them which I could give overseas troops at the Jamboree as coming from myself. Could you spare time to come here (and spend the night if you like) and have a look at them. Mr. Eggar also would like your opinion as to whether bends for bows could be made from them.

Don did carve some totems for the World Jamboree (1929), which were about six feet high, although in the Scout Magazine they were described as being made from 1200 year old oak rather than yew.[7] The totems were presented by Baden-Powell to five 'British Dominions'. On the back of each Don had carved, in the style of Baden-Powell's handwriting, the words: 'Friendship. Jamboree, 1929. R.B.-P'.

Each totem animal which Don carved was particularly significant to that country. In general, the inspiration for his carvings came from either one of Rudyard Kipling's *Jungle Books* or were mythical creatures from other cultures. He mostly carved direct, but sometimes would make a clay sketch-model to begin with. The last totem he carved was many years after he left Gilwell. This was in response to a specific request from the Wolf Cubs of the 1st Newington Scout Group. For sentimental reasons and because of his 'attachment to Newington' he found he 'couldn't resist' and 'carved the best totem that he had ever done - and the last!'[8] For the totem he carved the *Jungle Book* figures of Akela, the Bunderlog, Mowgli and the frog.

[11] Totem poles carved by Don

# Gidney Memorial Log Cabin

Today at Gilwell one can still see several constructions made by Don. They range from the physically massive Gidney Memorial Log Cabin [12, 13] to a series of fine carvings on the cupboard panels in the dining room.

[12] Gidney Memorial Log Cabin: early stages of construction. Don standing in the interior

[13] Gidney Memorial Log Cabin finished: exterior and interior

# The Leopard Gates

In 1928, Don constructed and carved the main entrance gates for Gilwell. These heavy, wood-hewn trellis gates are topped by a pair of crouching leopards. In 1996, when Don last visited Gilwell at the age of ninety-four, he noted that one of the animals was missing [14]. Returning home, he set about carving a replacement, so now the main gates once more have a pair of leopards.

## Jim Green Gate

Don also built and carved the Jim Green Gate (1930) which is a memorial lych gate with a thatched roof [15, 16, 17]. Jim Green was once the Editor of the Scout's National Magazine, *The Scouter,* and died tragically young. His father, Charles Dymoke Green, was the Scout Association's Secretary.

[14] Original *Leopard,* 1928, carved by Don

[15] Don constructing the Jim Green Gate with Colonel Belge Wilson looking on

[16] Don carving the Gilwell 'Axe and Log' symbol

[17] Jim Green Gate with thatched roof

[15]

[16]

[17]

# Rope Spinning

While at Gilwell, Don developed expertise in perhaps one of the more surprising skills of his life: this was how to use a lariat (a lasso) and a spinning rope. After seeing a rope-spinning performance by a cowboy named Tex McLeod in a London theatre (c. 1920). Don went backstage to meet him. There and then, McLeod taught Don his first rope tricks. Completely fascinated by the art, Don gave McLeod an open invitation to visit Gilwell. This McLeod did and Don reports that 'at the end of a year [he] had become very skilful with the ropes, but it took much longer to be at ease and cope with an audience'. There was a gradual demand to give roping shows and invitations came in from not only Britain, but France, Ireland, Holland [19] and Denmark. In Holland, Don met up with a Dutch friend he had made at Gilwell. This was Titus Leeser [18] who, like Don, became a much-respected sculptor. In Holland, Leeser carried out many architectural commissions for churches which had been damaged or destroyed in World War II. Many years later both worked on the Bryanston War Memorial (see page 178).

There are a few seconds of film showing Don demonstrating rope-spinning at Gilwell when the Prince of Wales made a visit in 1926. Unfortunately, the Prince had to leave early thus missing the demonstration. In a letter to Don concerning this event Baden-Powell wrote[9]:

> I hear that you surpassed yourself in the rope spinning before the American Ambassador. I am only so sorry that the Prince had to leave so early and could not stay to see it: but I hope he will come another day to do Gilwell quietly and then to see you at it. I showed him your handiwork at the Scouts Camp Fire. He was very taken with it.

Another keen rope-spinner at Gilwell was Francis Gidney who:

> practised for hours and hours until he was expert. His companion in this was Don Potter, whose skill is, or was, well known. Don had also to endure other experiments such as the stockwhip; only his devotion to Gidney could have made him endure the many flicks he got with the whip as Gidney tried to bring off various tricks. Then there was knife-and-axe-throwing; at least one fine tree at Gilwell was brought to an early death by this experiment. B-P at last stepped in and forbade both the use of the stockwhip and axe-throwing as activities for boys.[10]

[18] Don with Titus Leeser in Holland

[19] Don rope spinning in Holland

Don certainly became something of a celebrity performer. He remembers taking part in a Wild West Rodeo at Wembley Stadium and appearing in Ralph Reader's Gang Show at the Albert Hall. 'Also, a startling performance in the East End of London at the Popular Hippodrome, where the manager, unbeknown to me, put in a line of dancing chorus girls as a background!'[11]

On April 1st 1928, Don performed at a Scouts' Rally in honour of Their Majesties, the King and Queen of Afghanistan, at the London Drill Hall, Buckingham Gate. In 1930, he was invited to write a chapter on how to use a lariat in *Rope Spinning* by D.W. Pinkney. The book has a photograph of Don on the front cover and another one accompanying the chapter.

Later in life, when teaching at Bryanston, Don was often called on to give rope spinning demonstrations for end-of-school entertainments. As one pupil, Michael Gill,[12] remembers: 'He would get two of us to run across the stage as fast as we could and would catch us both in one noose and bring us down with a thump!' Another pupil, Quin Hollick[13], claims that Don told him he lost his favourite raw hide lasso on a pony in the New Forest' However, Don continued rope spinning well into his nineties.

Besides Bryanston, Don would also give rope demonstrations at other schools, including Dane Court Prep School which was nearby. Dane Court had re-located from Pyrford to Whatcombe House in the Winterborne valley due to the Second World War. Richard Batterham[14] and Richard Bawden[15], both then young pupils at the School, remember Don's visit. "It was a roping display on the lawn…..we were all sitting around, there were only forty of us…and he lassoed me!" (Batterham). Don then got them to run about 'like cattle which he caught and tied up' (Bawden).

From Gilwell to Bryanston, Don's skills with a rope served him well and gave much pleasure to innumerable audiences. However, by the end of the Twenties, Don was feeling restless. Having gained impressive, if self-taught, expertise in wood-carving, he felt a growing need to learn how to carve stone. Sally Croome, daughter of 'Tiny' Chamberlain,[16] who at one time led the training programme at Gilwell, remembers that her family benefited from Don's early stone sculpture trials:

> My father created a rockery each side of the steps leading from our garage to the front door. For stones, he used Don's cast-off or rejected bits of women's busts and hips, so that I was able to go up to the house not using the steps, but jumping from a sculpted bust to a half-finished bottom!'

While giving lasso and rope spinning demonstrations in Britain and abroad, Don took every opportunity to visit art galleries and museums. He was, in particular, 'a great fan' of the V&A Museum. Finally, in 1930, he made the decision to leave Gilwell. However, for many years afterwards he responded to requests from The Scout Association for roping demonstrations. In 1936, Claude Fisher[17] in an article about Don for *The Rover World*, wrote:

> For ten years or more Don was the most sought-after Rover in all Britain…There can be few men with a greater number of friends - and they in almost every land.

A circle of friends that was to continue growing even wider throughout the years.

# Sculpture Commissions from The Scout Association

## Brownsea Island Commemorative Stone

Many years after Don left Gilwell he was given three major commissions by The Scout Association. The first was for a commemorative stone [20] to mark the place where Baden-Powell had held the first Scout Camp on Brownsea Island, from the 1st-9th August, 1907.[18] The camp site was on the south-west shore of Brownsea Island and looked across to the Purbecks. The commemorative stone is of Portland stone and is 2.7 metres high (nine feet). Don spent some considerable time choosing the rough stone from a Portland quarry before shaping and polishing it for lettering. The commission took about three months from start to finish. Don remembers it being 'quite a difficult one'. On one of the narrow edges of the stone Don created a textured surface, leaving a smooth relief form, the horn of a Greater Kudu, one of Africa's largest antelopes. Baden-Powell used such a horn when camping at Gilwell, sounding out long blasts to awaken the campers. The stone was unveiled on Brownsea island by Baden-Powell's daughter, Mrs. Betty Clay.

[20] Brownsea Island Commemorative Stone

[21] Baden-Powell Portrait-Bust carved for the Dominican Republic

## Baden-Powell Portrait-Bust for the Dominican Republic (1958)

The second Scout commission came from the Dominican Republic. This was the first country to commission a commemorative sculpture of Baden-Powell. The site chosen was Park Ramfis, one of the principal squares in the Dominican capital, Ciudad Trujillo. This portrait-bust [21] is one and a half times real life-size and weighs 15cwt.[19] Don carved it from a one-ton block of granite which came from the De Lank Quarry at St. Breward in Cornwall. The stone from this quarry is one of the world's hardest stones, which presents technical difficulties for any sculptor trying to carve it. It is a fine silver grey colour (it was used to build the Eddystone Lighthouse). Don carved the portrait-bust about sixteen years after he left Gilwell. He was then on the teaching staff of Bryanston School. Brinsley Tyrrell[20], a pupil at that time, remembers Don carving:

> the huge granite statue. My amazement that each chisel only lasted a few minutes before it needed re-sharpening by a blacksmith. He had fifty chisels and had to take them to the blacksmith every day. I recently carved a huge brain as part of a work, I remembered Don and used sandstone instead of granite, but I still used 50 chisels and had to have them sharpened and tempered every other day.

For the portrait, Don worked from photographs. He also enlisted the help of Baden-Powell's grandson, who came and sat for him - the grandson has a very similar bone structure to his grandfather. Once the sculpture was finished, it was taken to Southampton and shipped to the Dominican Republic. Today, Brownsea Island has the half-size sketch-model which is set into the outside wall of Brownsea Castle, a few yards from the quayside.

# Baden-Powell Sculpture for Baden-Powell House, London

The third commission from The Scout Association was for a 2.7 metre (nine feet) figure of Baden-Powell for Baden-Powell House, Queen's Gate, Kensington [22]. The stone which Don selected was, once again, Cornish granite from the De Lank Quarry on Bodmin Moor. Hedley Methven, a mason at the quarry, initially helped Don rough out the Baden-Powell figure [25, 26]. Methven was a native of St. Breward, his father and forefathers having all worked at the De Lank Quarry[21]. To begin with, Don and Methven worked in one of the quarry sheds, however, they created so much dust they were forced by the other quarrymen to re-locate themselves, and their stone, outside.

Information from The Scout Headquarters' Archives[22] gives some idea of the scale of the whole project:

> In order to produce a flawless block of granite, large enough for the purpose, it was necessary to quarry a piece weighing 14 tons [23]; this piece was then reduced to an oblong block weighing 6

[22] Baden-Powell sculpture outside Queen's Gate, London

tons [24]. The Sculptor already having submitted clay sketch models to the General Purposes Committee then produced a quarter-scale stone carving and it was from this that work on the oblong block began using tungsten tipped drills. When the block had been reduced to $3\frac{1}{2}$ tons it was transferred to the Sculptor's studio at Blandford Forum where the work was completed. From the 6-ton stage to completion took about 14 months.

On 12th July, 1961, Baden-Powell House, at Queens Gate, London, was opened by Queen Elizabeth II, accompanied by the Duke of Edinburgh. The figure of Baden-Powell was unveiled by The Duke of Gloucester. At the unveiling Don wore a suit and bow tie. He recalls that later he was 'ticked off for not wearing Scout uniform'!

[23] Quarrying a fourteen ton block of granite

[24] Oblong granite block weighing six tons

[25] Hedley Methven working with tungsten drill

[26] Hedley Methven and Don Potter at De Lank Quarry

## The Search for a Master

Having made the decision to leave Gilwell it took Don some time to secure an apprenticeship with a sculptor of his choosing. The one thing he was certain of was that he did not wish to study at the Royal Academy Schools; instead, he wanted to work with a Master, in his studio, 'as it has always been in the best periods of creative art'. He also wanted to carve stone rather than learn techniques of modelling. Mary Spencer Watson (a sculptor and life-time friend of Don's) has confirmed that in the early Thirties: 'there wasn't a chisel, piece of wood or stone in the whole of the Academy Schools'. She was fortunately allowed to exchange places with a student at the Central School of Art. This meant she could carve direct in stone. In the early 1920s, Don also attended the Central School. However, this was for Life Drawing to which he went one day a week for a term.

At the Central in 1936, there were teachers such as Alfred Turner and John Skeaping. Skeaping had been married to Barbara Hepworth but as Hepworth later wrote: 'quite suddenly we were out of orbit…we fell apart.'[1] 'Through Hepworth, Skeaping was very much in touch with all the young bloods, including Henry Moore'.[2] From a studio in Hampstead, Moore put together his first one-man show (1931) for the Leicester Gallery in London, and asked Epstein to write the preface for the exhibition catalogue.

# The years with
# Eric Gill

# Meeting with Epstein

Epstein was the first sculptor Don approached. Born in 1880 and then fifty-one years of age, this avant-garde sculptor had won a high, if somewhat notorious reputation for his work. As a young student at the turn of the twentieth century he had studied in Paris, a city which then deemed Auguste Rodin to be its leading contemporary sculptor and Aristide Maillol its rising star. The modelled work of Rodin was regarded by the Parisian Art Establishment to be exemplary. This, however, was before the scandal of the 'faux Rodin', when it was revealed that Rodin's clay models were reproduced by a pointing machine which allowed replicas to be made by technicians.

Towards the end of his life, however, Rodin also faced a challenge which came from 'the highly reductive carved sculpture of Constantin Brancusi'.[3] This sculptor, along with Epstein, Modigliani, Zadkine and others, gave a commitment to direct carving rather than modelling. They were interested in archaic, rather than classic works; they studied carvings from Egypt, Assyria and early Greece. They also looked to African and Oceanic carvings. In sympathy with such indigenous, un-tutored work, they too chose to carve direct into the block. Sometimes they worked from a clay or stone sketch model, rarely from a drawing. As Spencer Watson relates:

> Epstein wanted to break down this awful, emaciated copy of the Renaissance that was going on. All these academic sculptors who carved beautifully, although they were Scandinavian, they were still sweet, Renaissance tradition, nothing to do with Mexico or Babylonia or any of these lovely 'crude' carvings.

However, after some years of direct carving, in the 1920s, Epstein returned to modelling and produced a number of portrait busts. He modelled original portraits in clay but then handed the sketch models over to a technician to be cast in bronze. In doing so, many felt Epstein was compromising his status as someone who worked directly with his material.

Epstein's change to modelling may have been induced by his need to secure a better income as his stone sculptures were continuing to arouse antagonism from the public. *Jacob and the Angel*, now in the Tate Britain, 'were exhibited in a side show at Blackpool as the most frightening things the visitor was likely to see'.[4] Many of his bronzes did not fare much better. His *Risen Christ* [1920] was described 'as a horror in bronze….with his Bolshevik appearance'.[5] Spencer Watson certainly remembers Epstein's bronzes as being 'almost too alive, there was demonic life in them…it almost destroyed them

[27] *Indian Head Shield*

as works of art. They were <u>so</u> like the people they were almost a caricature.'

By the time Don met Epstein, in 1931, the sculptor was producing both bronzes and carvings in stone - *Night and Day* was carved in 1929 and *Genesis* in 1931. As a possible Master for a young apprentice, Spencer Watson has said she can well 'suppose a young man like Don would have gone to Epstein: 'His craftsmanship, his figures and portraits were brilliant, absolutely brilliant.' Initially, Don wrote asking for an appointment, but receiving no reply he decided 'to brave the lion's den'. When he rang the door bell, Epstein invited him in. Don recalls that Epstein 'melted after a bit, especially when he said he liked *Rima*[6]. Epstein praised Don's work; he particularly liked his totem pole, although he was not so keen on his carved shield [27]. Ultimately, however, the chemistry between the two did not work. Epstein was certainly not an easy man. The meeting, though, did inspire Don, and in the following months he became determined to find a Master he could work with. Frank Dobson [1886-1963] was a credible alternative to Epstein, but Don did not feel the same attraction to Dobson's carving. Spencer Watson has described Dobson as: 'trying to do big form stuff, not pretty, pretty……the big solid, female figure…all your form had to go round…..he was very good, he'd got all the right ideas, but he wasn't the demonic genius of Epstein'. In the 1920s, Dobson received much critical acclaim for his work: Roger Fry and Clive Bell admired his 'soft and broad-limbed classicism'.[7] However, Dobson's increasing alliance to the Maillol tradition did not inspire either Don or Spencer Watson.

# Don's Approach to Eric Gill

Spencer Watson has said that:

> by 1931, Epstein, Hepworth, Moore and Gill, and Armitage a little later, were all having shows at the Leicester Gallery in Leicester Square. We all used to go, as a little critical bunch of students, and look at these masters' works - a very interesting time - but Gill was the old master, he <u>was</u> a master, and of course Don went to Gill. His craftsmanship was immaculate, his ability with stone was fantastic, beautiful.

Walter Ritchie, who became, like Don, an apprentice to Gill, wrote that 'Henry Moore was to make his millions with his bronze reproductions but Gill in his relative poverty possessed a magic of far greater complexity.'[8]

It was on the initial advice of Josh Reynolds, that Don first wrote to Gill. Gill was certainly regarded as something of a prophet by the younger generation. For him, stone carving 'wasn't just doing things in stone…..it was conceiving things in stone and conceiving them as made by carving'.[9] He used local, native stone - Hoptonwood, Portland - rather than Italian marble and in his book, *Art and a Changing Civilisation* (1934), he argued that the artist must <u>first</u> be a craftsman and that carving was the 'type of the craft of the sculptor'. Carving was what sculptors did rather than make clay models for technical assistants to either enlarge and cut in stone or copy and cast in bronze.

Carving was also more than architectural masonry: it was <u>sculpture</u>. Working direct with stone and its natural properties was part of the craftsman's art and part of the challenge. The block offered its own resistance; changes could not easily be made: 'there is no putting back tomorrow what was cut away today'.[10] Such direct engagement gave an excitement and honesty to the sculptor's work - and original ideas might well be transformed and enhanced into something new.

Describing Gill's method of working, Don has written that:

> Gill …carved by the archaic Greek technique of end-pointing - using the point at right angles to the stone. [He used] the usual stone carver's points, claws and flat chisels. He also used a bouchard or bush-hammer which is a hammer with two square-section striking ends divided into pyramid shaped points. Repeated blows reduce the stone by slow pulverisation.[11]

For Gill, who originally was in sympathy with William Morris, the division between art and craft became artificial. His own training had been in Lettering at the Central School of Arts & Crafts with Edward Johnston, and also, on the advice of the Principal, W.R. Lethaby, in masonry (see page 172). Gill's first stone sculpture, *Estin Thalassa*, was not exhibited until 1910, but was then highly praised by critics such as Roger Fry, Count Kessler and William Rothenstein. In 1928, Gill showed at the Goupil Gallery Exhibition along with sculptors such as Rodin, Maillol and Gaudier-Brzeska. Ritchie has written that Lord Howard de Walden 'gave Gill the use of his ballroom in London to carve *Mankind* and other works for [this] important exhibition.'[12] Exhibiting in such distinguished company meant that at last Gill had consolidated his public position as a major sculptor in Britain.

# Don's first meeting with Eric Gill

When Don first wrote to Gill in 1931, he was more than aware that he was approaching a quite formidable practitioner. With his letter, Don sent some photographs of his work, the result of which was that Gill sent him an invitation to meet outside the front entrance of BBC Broadcasting House in Langham Place. There Gill was working on the BBC commission of *Prospero* and *Ariel*: 'some finishing was necessary after the sculpture was hoisted into position - working off joints etc.'[13] Moving such a sculpture from Pigotts, where Gill lived and worked, had been no mean task: 'Pigotts Hill was beautiful but it was a 1:6 curse to heavily laden lorries and access to the workshops was not ideal [28].'[14]

Don's interview with Gill took place at the top of some high scaffolding. Gill was dressed in clothes somewhat redolent of those worn by medieval craftsmen. Don has described Gill's usual wear as being:

[28] Pigotts Driveway

a simple handwoven tunic or smock with a leather belt, woollen stockings, shoes and a beret. The tunic would be a dark colour for daywear but he would change into a light, perhaps natural colour for evening. For stone carving he wore a square paper hat which he folded out of a newspaper, like an old-fashioned carpenter's hat.

After the interview they both adjourned to a neighbouring café to talk further. Gill offered Don a six months' trial after which, Don says: 'nobody noticed when the time was up and I stayed for six years'. Even after this, Gill continued to pass on wood carving commissions to Don. This only ceased in 1940 with Gill's death.

## Gill's assistants and apprentices

Over a working life-time, Gill had about twenty-seven assistants, apprentices or pupils; each of whom stayed on average for about a year. Don's association with Gill was longer than that of any other pupil or apprentice besides the Cribb brothers, whom Gill regarded as his 'anchor men'.

Don was the first new apprentice Gill took on at Pigotts. He arrived just when Gill had made a decision to enlarge his workshops to keep up with a growing demand for his work. This demand seemed to co-incide with Gill's recent move from Capel-y-ffin in a remote part of Wales, to 'leafy Bucks' with High Wycombe 'only four miles down the valley'[15] and London a short journey away on the train. Don's arrival, however, also co-incided with Gill's poorer state of health, which after 1930 was never robust again.

Amongst the apprentices and assistants at Pigotts whom Don particularly remembers were Laurie Cribb, Walter Ritchie, Angus McDougall (son of the psychologist, William McDougall), Anthony Foster, David Kindersley, Hew Lorimer and John Skelton (Gill's nephew).

# Walter Ritchie

Most of the quotations from Don in this chapter are taken from Don's book: *My Time with Eric Gill: A Memoir by Donald Potter* (1980). The book was designed and published by Walter Ritchie [1919-1997] in a limited edition of five hundred. It was during a visit to see Don at Bryanston, that Ritchie was shown the original manuscript. Don was then about seventy-eight. Ritchie decided to publish the book because he felt he owed Don 'such a lot'[16] and because the book would be a fitting tribute to the man and his work.

In the addenda to the book, Ritchie writes of his first meeting with Don in 1938. By the late Thirties, Don had left the Gill workshops at Pigotts to set up on his own nearby. However, Gill continued to send him work and Ritchie used to act as Eric Gill's messenger. He writes that:

> any feeling of irritation at being taken away from my work was soon dispelled by the field walk to Speen and the anticipation of seeing what was going on in Donald's studio.

Ritchie first came to work with Gill in 1938 because he was attracted by his 'concern with life and religion; [Gill] had come to sculpture through architecture and lettering and he worked on buildings.' Ritchie's own future interests lay in town planning and urban regeneration. He completed many public architectural projects, believing that art should be 'more human and part of everyday life, not exclusive to galleries but placed where it is relevant to locality'. It should also 'reflect the individuality of the person or persons commissioning as much as the artist creating it'.[17] . *Hands* is a very early carving from 1939 [29].

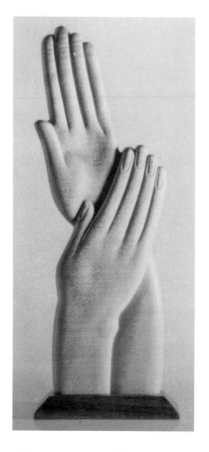

[29] *Hands*. Carving by Walter Ritchie, 1939

While at Pigotts, Don gave much support to this young apprentice, as Sally Taylor,[18] a life-long friend of Ritchie's, relates:

> Walter had come from Art school in Coventry to Eric Gill. He stayed with Gill for about a year. He was very shy but very committed. Don had a way of making him feel less shy. He learnt a lot about wood carving from Don who also introduced him to classical music. Don once put him on the back of his motorbike with his cello and they went to a friend's [Dora McAttan] house. She had a gramophone and they listened to Beethoven's Seventh Symphony. For Walter it was a wonderful experience of listening and listening properly. It left him with a love of classical music.

Ritchie left Pigotts in 1939. As a conscientious objector he had no wish to attract the attention of the police and war-time authorities to Gill's stance on pacifism. Later, both Ritchie and Don spoke of Gill's 'magnetism'. Although neither agreed with Gill about many matters (Don particularly about Roman Catholicism), they both found him to be encouraging, generous and kind.

# Pigotts

Gill's establishment at Pigotts [30] consisted of a set of red-brick eighteenth century buildings in a quadrangular setting. Don has described the lay-out as thus:

Gill's workshop and his engraving room were on the east side; Denis Tegetmeier and the apprentices on the west, printing rooms on the north and living quarters and cottages on the south, with a pigsty and the two pigs in the middle. A string with a tin can on the end went across the courtyard from Gill's workshop to the apprentices and we would know from the number of pulls who was being summoned.

In the corner where Pigott's farmhouse met Gill's workshop, Gill sited a Chapel which became licensed for Mass:

Gill belonged to a Roman Catholic religious order - the Dominican Tertiaries - officiated over by a resident priest, and certain disciplines were observed, one of which was the singing of the Angelus…when we were all supposed to stop work and say a short prayer.

However, as Robert Speaight[19] has written, 'the piety at Pigotts was less obtrusive than at Ditchling' (Gill's former home between 1907 and 1924); it was also 'infinitely more accessible than Capel'. One major contributing difference to the atmosphere at Pigotts was the diffusing presence of apprentices, such as Don, who were not Roman Catholic.

Of family members living at Pigotts, besides Gill and his wife, Mary, Don remembers their adopted son, Gordian, and Gill's two married daughters, Petra and Joanna. The daughters lived with their respective husbands and children in separate living quarters. Petra was married to Denis Tegetmeier, the painter, engraver and designer, and Joanna, to René Hague who ran the printing press at Pigotts. Betty, the Gill's third daughter, lived in Wales. She was married to David Pepler but subsequently widowed. Her children attended May Reeves' school at Pigotts during term time. Two other permanent but non-family members at Pigotts were 'the odd job man, Charlie, who drove the car and looked after the animals (one cow, one sheep and two pigs)' and 'Fred, the gardener, a great character who lived in the next village.'[20]

Don remembers life at Pigotts being quite orderly:

We started work about nine and Gill would usually come over to us an hour later after dictating his letters for Mary to write out in her neat script. He would look at our progress and pass comments, giving advice or allocating new work. After that he would retire either to his engraving room or to his carving workshop and unless we were helping him, we wouldn't see much of him until tea time when we would gather together in his workshop and eat Mary's wonderful home-made bread, baked in a primitive oven. Tea finished, out would come his old Oxo tin full of tobacco, with EG engraved on the lid, and he would roll himself a cigarette and chat for a while, then we would return to work until about six o'clock.

# Elizabeth Taylor

The Coles family were local neighbours of the Gills'. The daughter, Elizabeth (1912-1975), became a regular visitor to Pigotts and did some life-modelling for Gill. A youthful romantic attachment arose between Don and Elizabeth and in 1933 Elizabeth wrote a poem [31] dedicated to D.P.[21]

[31] Origin to D. P.
Elizabeth Coles

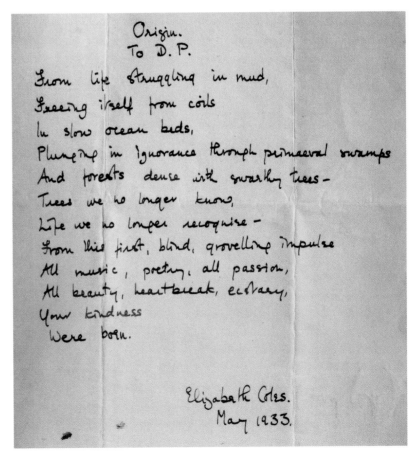

Elizabeth Coles later married and took her husband's surname of Taylor. She became a celebrated author and altogether, eleven novels and five volumes of her short stories were published. When Virago Modern Classics re-published her work they classed her as the Jane Austen of this century: a writer who worked 'with a small canvas', but always 'wonderfully observed, witty, yet profound' (1985).[22]

Elizabeth Bowen, a contemporary author, wrote to Taylor praising her novel: *The Wedding Party*, first published in 1968. She found that the book 'obsessed' her and she wrote: 'What I think is great is to have such a celerity in the action, such a moment-to-moment actuality about the surface'.[23] The novel was in fact a thinly-disguised and somewhat satirical account of Eric Gill and Pigotts. It concerns a self-sufficing community in which, it must be stressed, Don does not appear!

The story is about an artistic colony at Quayne, presided over by Henry Bretton, who along with his whole family, has converted to Roman Catholicism. They have their own chapel and a resident priest. At dinner in the evenings, Bretton reads aloud or 'pontificates'. The insular-looking women garden, cook, weave and scrub. The daughters, with husbands and children, live in farm cottages adjacent to the main farmhouse and courtyard. The whole account is unremittingly harsh, only the apprentices in the workshop escape Taylor's 'bite'. MacCarthy (1989) has conjectured that Taylor wrote the novel in retaliation for Gill showing Count Kessler (with whom he was staying in 1931), John Rothenstein, and others, some life-drawings he had made of her.[24]

While at Pigotts, Gill did indeed use many life-models, who were mostly either friends or relatives. He had a room at the far end of the workshop for drawing. Here both Daisy Hawkins, the housekeeper's daughter, and May Reeves, who lived in a caravan in the orchard, posed for him. As Speaight has written: 'Auntie May' - as she was called - ran a school at Pigotts for the Hague and Tegetmeier children.'[25] It is generally accepted that Gill had affairs with both Daisy and May.

Although Gill's establishments tended to be somewhat enclosed communities, they also welcomed selected visitors. Some were priests from the Dominican Tertiaries, others were artists, friends and writers. They included Stanley Morison and Beatrice Warde from Monotype Corporation; the potter, Bernard Leach from St. Ives; Jim Ede, Assistant-Director of the Tate Gallery and founder of Kettle's Yard at Cambridge; Herbert Read, the art critic; G.K. Chesterton, the author and poet, and David Jones, painter and poet.

# David Jones

David Jones (1895-1974) stayed a good deal at Pigotts and indeed was engaged for some years to Petra, Gill's second daughter. Don came to know Jones during this time. For a period of four years, from 1928, Jones drew and painted many watercolours at Pigotts. These paintings became increasingly floating and transparent, seeming to emerge from the visionary world of Blake. Among his subjects were: *Eric Gill* (1930); *René Hague's Press* (1930); *Pigott's Farmyard* (1930); *The Long Meadow* (1932); and *The Farm Door* (1937). He also once sketched Don playing the cello but alas, as Don recalls, he has not seen the drawing since that day. The sketch was made on one of the evenings when Gill invited Don to bring in his cello and play Corelli sonatas with him. Don recalls Gill playing a 'rather tinkling spinet' and says that overall, Gill's taste in music strongly centred on 'music of the Plain Chant age'.

One other particular memory Don has of Jones was when the latter was 'idling away in the workshop one evening and absent-mindedly sketched a woman' on the back of a piece of stone. Gill liked the sketch so much that he carved it on the back of the stone for *Prospero*, the BBC commission. Today, Don affirms, the carving is still there: 'a beautiful linear carving of a nude woman about 18'' high which is unlikely to ever be seen by anyone'.

# Wood Carvings for Gill

When Don first arrived at Pigotts he brought with him a totem; this was a commission from Baden-Powell which was still outstanding. MacCarthy has speculated that the totem must have stood out rather incongruously in a workshop surrounded by Catholic iconography.[26]

Gill, although a wood engraver, was not a wood carver. He once told Don that carving a large altarpiece for Rossall School Chapel had given him dreadful sleepless nights. Gill felt stone lent itself naturally to sculpture, but wood only reluctantly. Don of course disagreed, having an instinctive feeling for wood. While at Pigotts, Don carved an oak crucifix for Gill which 'was placed high in a tree in the beech woods which surrounded Pigotts on three sides. This tree and its sculpture was the destination of Eric's daily walk.'[27]

A very short time after Don started at Pigotts, Gill began passing on his wood carving commissions to him. Don has said 'it got to the pitch so that Gill would do me a rough sketch and say, "Carve that in wood".' This suited Don, for his interest 'lay with carving wood in the round [rather than] engraving on the flat,

[32] *Owl* newel post height 62cm (24¹/2'') Winchester College

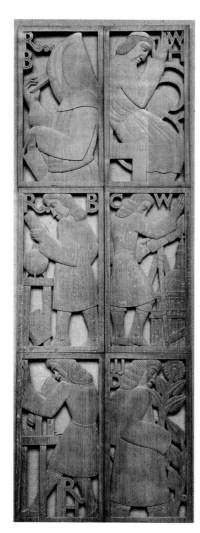

[33] Radcliffe Science Library Carving, 1935

in one dimension'. *St. Sebastian* [36], which is in the Library of Winchester College, was carved in 1933. Don worked this exquisite carving from a light pen-wash sketch by Gill. In an interview with Lucien Myers[28], in 1978, Don told Myers that at first, such carvings would be described as being by Eric Gill and Donald Potter. Later, however, he noticed that the Donald Potter tended to disappear from the titles. In his generous manner Don felt it was not too bad a bargain considering what he learned from Gill. The *Owl* [32], also in the Library at Winchester College, was also probably carved by Don at the same time.

## Radcliffe Science Library

One of the more intricate pieces of wood carving that Don completed for Gill was a commission from the Bodleian Library in Oxford, for the Radcliffe Science Library (1935). Don worked from some pencil sketches by Gill. The commission was for 'six pierced panels in doors to rare books' and was costed at £150.[29] Each panel depicts a scientist with an Oxford connection: Roger Bacon (top left), Robert Boyle (middle left), Robert Hooke (botton left), William Harvey (top right), Christopher Wren (Middle right) and J. J. Dillenius (bottom right) [33]. The doors, attributed to Gill are still in their original location, on the first floor of the 1934 (Worthington) wing of the Radcliffe Science Library. The room to which they gave access was originally the Rare Books Room, but is now the office of the Keeper of Scientific Books.

## Crucifixion for St. Peter's Church, Gorleston-on-Sea

Another Gill sketch [34] which Don worked from, was for the central altar crucifixion [35] for the Catholic Church of St. Peter the Apostle, Gorleston-on-Sea. Gorleston is near Yarmouth in Norfolk. Ritchie has written that the church was designed by Gill 'in collaboration with J.E. Farrell, an architect who lived quite close to Pigotts'.[30] It was designed from the starting point of a central altar. In 'Plain Architecture' Gill wrote that a church is there 'first and chiefly as a canopy over an altar'.[31] The church was dedicated in 1939, a year before Gill's death.

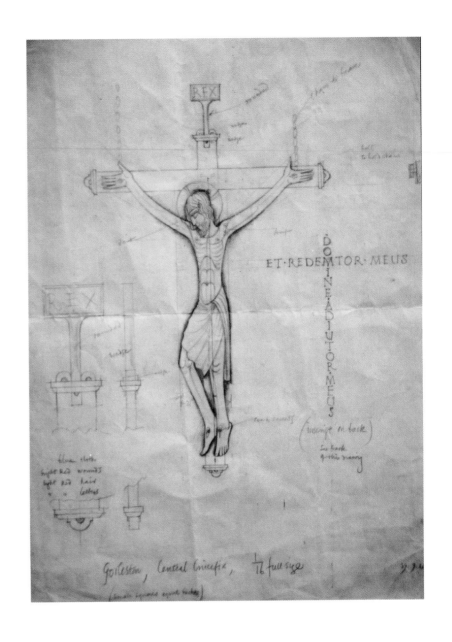

[34] Gorleston Crucifixion Eric Gill's
sketch

# Master/Pupil relationship

Gill rarely signed his work Indeed, many works which emerged from Gill's workshops were carved by either pupils or assistants. As a practice this was not highly unusual. Ritchie[33] once wrote that:

> Anthony Foster was a meticulous stone carver; George Friend hammered and chased Gill's designs in silver and Donald Potter, who has real feeling for wood, translated his drawings into this material.

Laurie Cribb, a superb mason and letter cutter, was perhaps Gill's most 'stalwart' assistant. It was from Cribb that Don learnt much about letter cutting (see page 174). Don recalls that at Pigotts, Gill left most of the lettering to Cribb: 'Gill used to come and draw it on the stone, slab or slate and then just leave it to Laurie.'

In retrospect, Ritchie wrote of his discomfort concerning the Master and Workshop regime. He argued that 'technique is soon absorbed by an intelligent pupil' and that in any 'group-working' each should have the recognition for their own finished work. He went on to say:

[36] *St Sebastian* height 1.52m (5 feet)
Walnut

It may not be sufficiently realised how great a debt a sculptor who adopts a delegated method of working owes to his assistants. Gill's life would have been very different without these men who freed him for his polemical activities of writing and lecturing, took much of the hard work from his sculpture and carried out most of his letter-cutting.[34]

As a consequence of his own experiences:

Ritchie designed and carved his work without any studio assistants [believing that] sculpture…should be an extension of mental processes that allow constant reassessment of the emerging form, an activity for which delegation should be unthinkable.[35]

Hilary Spurling's[36] comment has been that 'though his own work belied him, Gill believed in corporate identity, the suppression of the individual and the supremacy of anonymous craftsmanship.'

# Eric Gill as Teacher

In his book about his years with Eric Gill, Don wrote about Gill's views as a teacher. The following are a small selection of Gill's sayings:

the idea of students working in a Master's studio as in medieval and renaissance times…..he was contemptuous of art schools…..

When talking to us he would always use our Christian names but expected us to call him Sir, somewhat in perpetuation of that tradition…

We, his pupils, were to copy and learn all he had to show us and then improve on it, or take what we needed….

He taught more by example than words, although we got plenty of those as well…

He was very fond of mottoes and sayings, one of which was 'Bad workmen quarrel with their tools, because good workmen do not use bad tools' and 'An artist is not a special kind of man, but every man is a special kind of artist'[37]

Art should be for a definite purpose - not just art for art's sake……

[37] Don's first stone carving, 1931

From Gill, Don acknowledges that he learned much about stone carving and lettering - most came through observation:

> Gill would start …by concentrating on certain points - the position and rounding of a shoulder - the point of a bent knee - the position and curve of the belly - suggestion of breasts - the rounded top of the head etc. The result would look like Lot's wife in a pillar of salt! But the eye could easily travel from point to point and connect up the rest of the figure. After that it meant cutting away the surplus stone rather like peeling a banana.

> We learnt to respect the nature of our materials and impart to our sculpture that firm, crisp, stone-like quality seen in the best periods of carvings down the ages: he frequently quoted the carvings on Chartres Cathedral.

Don's first stone carving at Pigotts was a study for a life-size work in Portland stone, 1931 [37].[38]

## Sea Horses: Morecambe Hotel

In 1933, Gill received two commissions from the London, Midland and Scottish Railway for their hotel at Morecambe. Gill, who had a passion for steam trains, had already designed the nameplate for The Flying Scotsman. Of the Morecambe commissions one was for an indoor bas-relief carving: *Odysseus welcomed from the Sea by Nausicaa*; and the other, for a sculpture, *Sea Horses* [38], on the outside of the building.

Don accompanied Gill to carve the *Sea Horses* in Portland stone. He worked from a stone-sketch made by Gill. Initially he recalls that Laurie Cribb worked with him but then Gill took Cribb away to work on the lettering of the indoor panel which measured 4.57 x 2.13 metres (15 x 7 ft). The inscription which Cribb lettered read: 'There is no hope that thou may'st yet see thy friends'. Ironically, if rather sadly, while Gill was working at Morecambe, his father died and so Gill returned south for the funeral. Don remembers that Eric Ravilious also came to work with them.

[38] *Sea Horses* for Morecambe Hotel
Portland stone

## Working *in situ* with Gill

In Don's opinion, Gill was someone who could initiate 'an atmosphere of great vitality', although 'he could on occasion be caustic and cutting'. However, his was always 'a marked presence'. In particular, Don enjoyed his company when working *in situ* on an architectural carving:

Working with him in the restricted area of scaffolding - perhaps high above a busy London street, encouraged a more relaxed relationship:

> There was a time when we were working in a suburb of London on a large departmental store; the owner and Big Boss stood for all that Gill despised. One of the carvings to go on the front of this building was a large coat-of-arms about twelve feet square and there had been trouble about the tail of the prancing leopard in the crest - underneath was an inscription which translated into, 'I serve the right'. Unfortunately Laurie Cribb had cut the letters not quite in the middle of the scroll so Gill reached for his hammer and chisel and filled the gap with a grand flourish - the nearest thing to a question mark I've seen and there it stands to this day! [The coat of arms had in fact been commissioned for Bentall's store in Kingston-on-Thames].

# Last days at Pigotts

Whenever he was away from Pigotts, Gill would keep in touch with those at home. Don has several cards and letters from Gill, the first of which he received just two months after starting work with him. Postmarked Bristol (8.11.31), Gill wrote to Don hoping 'all goes well' and then signed it with his distinctive E, underscored G, signature.

In the Thirties, Gill became increasingly pre-occupied with literary matters or giving talks or lectures. He also travelled abroad. In 1934, he went to Jerusalem to carve ten panels for the New Archaeological Museum. The four months he spent working there had a visible effect on him. He felt his mind become 'pervaded by a different order of living...... an order not only human but essentially holy. [He saw there], as it were eye to eye, the sweating face of Christ'[39] and his antagonism to Europe's capitalist-industrial society and his support for pacifism grew even more.

During the autumn of 1936, Gill was unwell with an attack of bronchitis and congestion of the lung. He became so concerned with thoughts of death that he designed a gravestone for himself and asked Don to do the lettering. The stone inscription read: 'Remember Me, Eric Gill, Lapidari, Eheu Mihi (Woe is me)'. Later, however, with his health somewhat restored, Gill carved his own tombstone which more simply read: 'Pray for me, Eric Gill, Stone Carver 1882-1940'.

However, Gill's health did not really pick up and in December of 1936, Mary and he accepted an invitation from Desmond Chute[40] to spend a few weeks in Italy at the Villa Raffaele in Rapallo [39]. From the Villa they were able to walk up to the point at Portofino from where they could see Genoa in one direction and La Spezia in the other. It was from here that Gill wished Don 'A Happy Christmas & love from E.G.' The postcard was addressed to Don's home: 'Slab Castle'. During some of his years with Gill, Don lived in a tiny cottage at Speen which he affectionately named Slab Castle[40].

[39] *Portofino* postcard (1936)

[40] Slab Castle: Gill's greetings from Rapallo

[41] *Sphinx* postcard from Eric Gill

Unfortunately, not long after returning from Rapallo, Gill fell off a trestle at Pigotts and broke a rib while working on the League of Nations carving. However, a subsequent sojourn in Palestine and Egypt seemed to restore his health once more. He was especially thrilled by a visit to the Pyramids and sent Don a postcard (dated 20.6.37) with an image of a Sphinx on it [41]. On the back he wrote: 'I saw this famous person on June 8th!'

About this time Don made a final decision to leave Pigotts and set up on his own. To some extent, he still felt resentment from Gill for not converting to Catholicism, but he says: 'perhaps even more, I needed to sort out and digest thoroughly all that I had learned from Gill'. Don needed to work separately from Gill in order to escape Gill's strong, pervasive influence. As Malcolm Yorke[41] has written, even when Gill's hand had not 'touched a piece from his workshop… it would bear the strong imprint of his mind and teaching'. Thus, a month after Gill's return from Palestine, 'feeling much better for the holiday', he discovered that 'the bird [had] flown from [the] shop'. However, in a letter to Don[42], he said he quite understood, wished him well and suggested it would be good to meet in London some time if Don was not coming down to Pigotts for a while. He then set about trying to sort out their finances:

I am now dealing with arrears of letters and accounts etc. and am not clear how I stand with you. Do I still owe you anything? I expect I do, and on the other side I suppose there is a small account for the rent. If you have got information on these points please let me know. As far as I can see rent is due from January 1st till your departure, and it seems that there is a balance due to you on sales at the French Gallery Exhibition. Let us know if you are likely to be able to take on jobs every now and then. Perhaps we could meet. Yours, Eric G

It is difficult to know exactly how many commissions Don carried out for Gill. In between such commissions, apprentices, such as Don, were 'always encouraged to get their own work …… and had the use of the workshop for carrying them out'.[43] Striking out independently meant Don having to face even greater financial insecurity than he was presently experiencing. At that time he was receiving about thirty shillings a month from Gill. The common practice in the workshop had always been for Gill to pay apprentices either a weekly rate (unless they came on a grant), or pay them for actual pieces.

Although life was not to be easy, Don determinedly set out to 'shake off the touch of Gill' and to walk his own path. This he certainly did but he admits to being grateful that:

> Gill continued to keep an eye on me and curiously enough whenever I was short of work, along would come a message asking me to take on a carving commission for him.

If this had not been the case, Don surmises, he would have surely starved!

'Slab Castle', Don's home at Speen, had 'one room up, and one room down, with a well outside the back door'. The cottage rent was '3/6d a week'. Although Don's home was extremely small, he recalls he truly thought it to be a palace. The village of Speen is near High Wycombe in Buckinghamshire, just a few miles from Pigotts. It was in Speen's little cemetery, adjoining the Baptist Chapel that Eric Gill was buried in 1940.

## Friends and neighbours: Cecil Collins, Edmund Rubbra and Angus McDougall

Not far from Don in the village, a young painter and writer by the name of Cecil Collins (1908-1989), came to live with his wife, Elizabeth. The couple originally met when they were students at the Royal College of Art. Angus McDougall had also been a student at the same time. Now he lived close by and was an apprentice with Eric Gill. Also living at Speen was Edmund Rubbra, the composer, and his wife, Antoinette. McDougall and Don were no doubt the go-betweens through whom everyone became aquainted.

On marrying, the Collins had lived in London, but soon after they also rented Monk's Cottage, set in remote woods in Highwood Bottom near Speen. The amenities of Monk's Cottage were very sparse, similar to those of Slab Castle. The Collins had no electricity so they lit oil lamps at night to enable them to see to read.

# Don's Home at Speen 1931-1940

[42] *The Angel with Adam* 1950 oil on canvas 80cms x 61cms 31 1/2" x 24"[6]

In Patrick Reyntiens'[2] estimation, Cecil Collins became the greatest sacred painter since William Blake. Always an individual, intuitive painter, his work fell outside any identifiable genre. Julian Trevelyan once described him as 'a cat that walks by himself - prophetic, poetic [and] visionary.'[3] Collins was certainly a visionary painter, who, as Canon Walker,[4] a long-term friend of Collins', has said: 'manifested the reality of angels in paint'. For Collins, the angel was the archetypal figure of universality: 'the winged thoughts of the Divine Mind'[42].[5]

Although Collins said he was not conscious of any influence from William Blake or Samuel Palmer, there was in the Thirties a revival of interest in Romanticism and visionary invention. Painters such as Paul Nash and Graham Sutherland became part of an eclectic group of Neo-Romantics. None, however, delved to the same depths of spirituality as Collins.

It was shortly after Collins' first, successful one-man exhibition in London (1935), that the couple decided to live permanently at Speen. They moved to Springhill, another cottage in the village. Here, Collins painted his surrealist *Magical Images in the Process of Time* (1935). Measuring 74 x 114cm (29 x 45") it was an unusually large oil for Collins. Don remembers such a large work, but is unsure if it is this one, which was wedged behind the bed in which he once slept in the Collins' cottage. *Magical Images* was exhibited at the International Surrealist Exhibition in London in 1936. Herbert Read declared the exhibition to be 'the dawn of a new age' but Collins, listening to Read, thought, 'No it isn't. It's the sunset.'[7] Partly to get away from a now unwanted association with the

Surrealists, and also to 'discover <u>who</u> he was and <u>where</u> he was'[8] he decided to leave London and live full time at Speen.

Besides painting, Collins also had a deep feeling for music, and, as Canon Walker has suggested, it came to have a bearing on his art. He played the piano and was highly skilled in improvisation. For Don, Collins was someone to share a love of music with. However, Don also had another neighbour who was even more musical: this was the composer Edmund Rubbra (1901-1986).

Rubbra was taught composition by Gustav Holst, who at one time saw Rubbra as the natural successor to Vaughan Williams. In his lifetime Rubbra composed an impressive number of works, including eleven symphonies; concertos for viola, piano and violin; four string quartets; and a number of masses and motets. On some evenings, Don, Rubbra, and his wife, Antoinette, would play chamber music together. Don would play cello; Edmund, piano; and Antoinette, violin. The friends would also meet at The Plough, a local inn run by the daughter of the politician, Ramsey McDonald.

McDougall and the Collins shared a love of amateur dramatics. Canon Walker says that although at times Collins was hyper sensitive:

> he also had a great sense of humour and valued humour in others. For him, humour was part of the Paradisal life… of the imagination and spirit. He would say we were all far too serious and involved in our cerebral lives.

Don remembers Collins as 'a practical joker', with a distinctive brand of humour:

> Once, Cecil wrapped up Angus McDougall in brown paper and put him in a box. He then told his wife, Elizabeth, that he had a surprise for her. He said there was a lovely present at the cottage gate waiting for her. When he took her down, the parcel started wriggling and got the giggles. It was Angus!

Although Eric Gill had seen Collins' exhibition in London, the two men did not meet until McDougall brought the Collins to visit him at Pigotts. After that, Collins and Gill had some very lively debates and arguments about God. Neither man was a trained academic but both had a remarkable gift for words. Although Collins had a dislike of the Church, he was, in Canon Walker's words: 'a deeply spiritual, deeply religious man, with a profound reverence for Christ.' Rarely did Collins or Gill come to any religious agreement but, Collins did attribute to Gill 'more understanding of the desperate position of the creative mind in our time than most people in England'.[9]

Don tended to avoid religious debates with Gill but McDougall was less reticent. Don records that once, following an evening meal at Pigotts, Gill and McDougall entered into a:

> lengthy and heated discussion on religion. When the time came for Angus to make his departure Gill laughingly said, 'Well Angus, I hope you don't meet the Devil on the way home.' On going through the wood back to his cottage, in the black of the night, a great horned apparition loomed up on the footpath in front of him. Angus was prepared to fight for his immortal soul whether he believed in its existence or not but before the terrible conflict could begin, the 'Devil' departed as suddenly as it had appeared - with a great leap into the bushes bordering the path! There had been a 'boxed' stag hunt the day before and the animal had escaped.

# Don's supplementary teaching

As early as 1934, Don had to do some teaching to supplement his income; he 'couldn't live off work from sculpting and lettering'. Along with his sister, Dorothy, he shared responsibility for looking after their elderly father, who had become increasingly frail. Don's father moved into 'Slab Castle', but as it was so small, Don moved out and shared another cottage, Longyards, with Dorothy. Later again, Don moved to White Cottage. With no pension or social security income to help them support their father, Don had to find additional income. This he did through teaching.

While living at Longyards, Don built himself a workshop in a field which he rented from a local farmer. This wooden building still exists, if in a somewhat modified version. At the present time it is Richard Batterham's second potting shed at Durweston. At one time, Batterham said Don was 'going to have it down in the quarry at Winspit but then the quarry owner changed and they didn't want him to have it there.' When Don finally left Speen and went to Bryanston he took the shed with him and later used the floor of it to pack a ten foot stone sculpture going to Malawi[10]. Eventually the much reduced shed came to Batterham who has himself moved it three times…..a well travelled shed!

# Letters of Reference from Lord Baden-Powell and Eric Gill

When Don first began to look for teaching opportunities, he asked both Baden-Powell and Eric Gill to write him letters of reference. Both letters [43, 44] are reproduced here:[11]

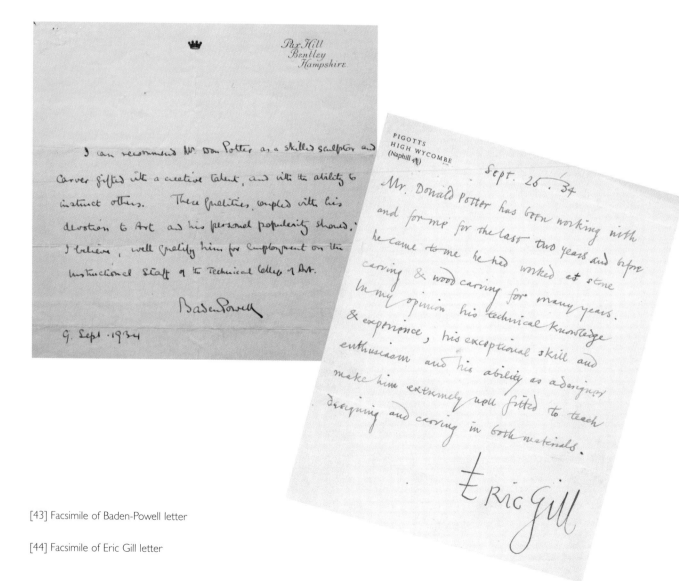

[43] Facsimile of Baden-Powell letter

[44] Facsimile of Eric Gill letter

# Oldfeld School, Swanage

The first school where Don taught was Hampden House, which Don's wife, Mary, recalls as being a prep school for girls. From there he went on to a part-time post at Oldfeld School, a Quaker preparatory school close to the beach in Swanage. The Headmaster was Arthur Hickson. Don used to travel from Speen to Swanage on his motorbike, carrying his cello in a soft case on his back. Once, just as he was heading for a dip in the road, 'a dog came running out from nowhere'. Don fell off, but was greatly relieved that the cello fell on top of him and so was not damaged!

While teaching sculpture at Oldfeld School [45], Don also supervised the building of a workshop, plus all its fittings. The labour came from volunteer school staff and pupils. He also built a stone archway in the garden of Hickson's home; the arch was an architectural feature to lead the garden visitor from one part of the garden to the next. It is still there. Don's teaching at Swanage came to an end when the School was forced to close and evacuate at the beginning of World War II. The Headmaster departed to Canada but, before leaving, highly recommended Don to T.F. Coade,[12] the Headmaster of Bryanston School. This introduction was to lead to perhaps one of the longest associations of any one teacher with any one school.

[45] Don at Oldfeld School, circa 1938 (Second from left: Keith Hickson; second from right: Thomas Hickson; other boys unidentified)

## Bryanston School and Don's Arrival

Bryanston School was once Portman House, the seat of the wealthy Portman family. Built in 1890, it is a huge red-brick construction architecturally dressed in Portland stone [46]. Built in a prominent position on a high chalk ridge it is aproned by acres of woodland. From a distance it presents a vision of a French chateau in an 'island' setting, indeed, the original design was 'borrowed' by Norman Shaw from Chateau Meran.[1]

From the grounds of Bryanston School there are views of the River Stour and Blandford Forum; the Shottsford Forum of Thomas Hardy. There are also views of soft chalk hills which stretch back to Winterbourne Stickland. Once, thousands of sheep, Hampshire Downs and Dorset Downs, were driven across this farmland to markets at either Blandford Forum or Sturminster Newton.[2]

Blandford Forum (which will here be referred to more familiarly as Blandford) is Bryanston School's nearest town. In its history it suffered from a number of fires, the last and most severe being in 1731. However, like the phoenix on John Bastard's pump and fire monument in the Market Place, the town valiantly rose again from its ashes. The town was completely rebuilt as Georgian and architecturally remains much the same. It is a well tempered place; coloured by buildings in red and mauve brick, flint, grey/green stone and cream plaster facings.[3]

Near to Bryanston School's main entrance, on the Dorchester road, there is a fine, stone bridge, built in 1783.[4] This Georgian bridge crosses the River Stour [47] which has rich meadow-land lying to one side, and a steep bank of wood to the other. This particular reach of the river was widened and

# Bryanston Years:
# 1941-1982

[46] Don outside the main entrance of Bryanston School

straightened by the Portman family; an action subsequently much appreciated by generations of School rowing eights. For Don, it must have been quite a daunting experience when, crossing the river for the first time, he rode under the arch and up the long school drive bordered on each side by thick woodland. Equally, the Headmaster might have just been a little taken aback by his new teacher arriving on a motorbike, with all his worldly possessions, including a cello, strapped on the back!

# Thorold Coade: Headmaster of Bryanston School

It was through Don's philosophy of 'letting things happen to you', that he came to be offered a teaching post at Bryanston School. Arthur Hickson, Don's previous Headmaster from Oldfeld School in Swanage, had recommended him to Thorold Coade, Headmaster of Bryanston School. Sir Terence Conran states that Bryanston in the forties:

> was a relatively new school in [his] day and was run, as it is now, on the American Dalton system....so we all had a tutor and the timetable was tailored to suit each student..... I was there during the time of the Second World War, and a number of the teachers were conscientious objectors. There was a wonderful atmosphere

in the place, Coade set the style. Although he had a rather austere academic appearance, underneath he didn't quite let anarchy rule - but there was well controlled anarchy under his direction. .....[he was] a particularly sensitive and creative chap, understood Don Potter and gave him the chance to be a free spirit.[5]

Don recognised that:

Coade was out to respect the individual, helping to develop the whole person and letting him grow up in his own time; encouraging the creative imagination through art, drama and the various crafts.[6]

Richard Batterham remembers that Coade would 'come down to the pottery quite often to show people around. If you were down there when you were meant to be outside, break time that sort of thing, he never turned a hair or got in touch with you afterwards'!

Coade also had a dry sense of humour, which Don appreciated. In an article for the school magazine, *Saga,*[7] Don relayed some of Coade's classic school-report remarks:

He's trying - very!

and the Chemistry report from Geoffrey Ordish:

I believe he plays the bassoon

also another about a boy who was renowned for cribbing:

He is still forging ahead

and another

His standard is always low but this term he has failed to reach it.

All accounts of Coade seem to testify to the high regard in which both he, and his wife, were held. Brinsley Tyrrell has written that he:

set a tone for the School which I totally understood. The last rule in the rule book said: A breach of Common Sense is a breach of the School rules.

Tyrrell had to deal with the disadvantage of being dyslexic (not then recognised for what it was). However, even in those early days, teachers such as John Royds would let him 'draw through History classes provided [he] answered every question that was fired at him correctly'.

Anthony Luttrell[8] (former pupil), has written that it was certainly a credit to Coade that he never gave a sign that Don's 'unconventional ways' concerned him:

> I think it was part of a semi-progressive Bryanston ethos that the school could include a teacher like Donald alongside the amazingly urbane, sophisticated and intellectual art teacher, Charles Handley-Reade. Maybe it was this unlikely combination which led the school, in my time, to produce people of some significance.

Handley Reade taught at Bryanston between 1947-49, succeeding Roger Hilton, who taught there for just over a year from April 1947 to July 1948. The only information from the School Archivist, Alan Shrimpton[9], concerning Hilton's year at the School, comes from a contemporary pupil who said, Hilton 'used to stroll into the Art Room late with a bottle of whisky in his pocket and a copy of the *Racing Times* under his arm and simply say: "Get on with it".' In contrast to this, Don's style of teaching seemed considerably more cultured, as Tyrrell relates:

> While I and other students carved he sat in a corner, dressed in a white smock with his hair down to his shoulders and wearing a paper hat and played the cello. I could not believe that school could be so relaxed and sensible.

Although Don became an Associate of the Royal Society of British Sculptors he was never a person who sought traditional academic qualifications. As a school boy, Batterham remembers:

> There used to be a school list of all the staff and most of them had Exhibition at Brasenose, Scholar of this and that with lots of letters after their names.....and then on the second page down, it just said D. Potter - sculpture, metal work, pottery, technical drawing.

# Willi Soukop: Don's predecessor

Originally, the sculpture post at Bryanston became vacant because Willi Soukop, the School's former (visiting) sculptor, had been interned by the Authorities as an alien. Born in Vienna in 1907, Soukop was an Austrian national. After a short time in internment Soukop was permitted to travel to Canada. He stayed here until he was able to negotiate his return to England.

Over a number of years, like Don, Soukop supplemented his income as a sculptor by additional teaching and other paid work. For example, he made masks for school plays; Glyndebourne Opera (March 1938); and for the exiled Jooss-Leeder Ballet Company from Essen in Germany. Soukop, who originally wanted to be a painter, studied at the Academy of Fine Art in Vienna before coming to England in 1934. Once here, he established a base for himself at Dartington Hall in Devon, where he met, and became friends with the potter, Bernard Leach, who subsequently taught him how to pot.

Soukop's first visit to Bryanston was in 1936. After an initial, successful visit he was invited to teach wood carving and clay modelling on a basis of ten-days teaching per term. His first workshop space was in the main school building, two storeys below ground and next to the boilers. He wrote in *Saga*[10] (the School magazine) that the space was coated in 'black coal dust' and lit unsympathetically by 'electric light all day long' It was not until 1938 that a new sculpture studio, in 'Mr. Bramall's old garage'[11] transformed the situation. This

[48] Don Potter Art School opening, October 1997

airier space meant that pupils no longer had to first acclimatize themselves to a closed, fine, dust-laden atmosphere.[12] The pottery, however, remained in the cellars and was still there when Don arrived. Today it is located in the Don Potter Art School which was opened by Don in October, 1997 [48].

Under Soukop many young talents emerged in the field of sculpture. However, as his presence at Bryanston was somewhat intermittent, both he, and the School, found it hard to sustain the skills and enthusiasm of the pupils. In spite of this, Don recalls that when he first arrived at Bryanston he judged the sculpture to be of a high standard.

## Don's first meeting with the Staff

In 1941, the School was suffering from the inevitable side-effects of war: their pupil numbers had decreased to a hundred and twenty pupils. Don remembers that after the Fall of France, many parents took their boys away and sent them to America, which they presumed to be a 'safe' country. One such evacuee was the future musician, Christopher Wellington. However, on Wellington's 'return from the U.S.A. in autumn, 1944', he found a healthier school with 'three hundred and thirty boys'. During the war years, staff pay was reduced and Don was required not only to teach sculpture, pottery and metalwork, but also art. He was assured that this additional subject was just for an interim period as the art mistress had just been killed in an air raid. The whole teaching situation must have seemed somewhat overwhelming, particularly as Don was being employed on a part-time basis! However, when he walked into the School Common Room for the first time, he admits he felt some relief in recognising some familiar faces. These faces belonged to six staff members who had attended Scout training courses at Gilwell.

## The Old Stables

To begin with, Don had a room in the main Portman building, but he soon moved to rooms above the Old Stables in the Portman Stable Block [49]. These rooms, in the hipped part of the roof, probably originally housed grooms and coachmen. The Portman Stables were built in the same materials as the main house, that is, of red brick with Portland dressed stone. The stable yard encloses a central quadrangle. Nearby are the Portman kitchens which once serviced the main house. These high ceiling kitchens became

[49] The Old Portman Stables

Don's studio. Their height allowed him to work on large architectural sculptures. Anne, Don's daughter, remembers that they:

> had a wonderful rich smell of damp stone and wood shavings. A colony of horseshoe bats lived in the roof. Sometimes before 'Exhibition Day' at Bryanston Don would get the boys that he was taking potholing in the Cheddar Gorge, to practise sailing down ropes from the top of the high roof of his studio after clambering through the bat ridden attics.

Close by the Portman stables there is St. Martin's Church and the Portman Chapel [50]. Once, while Don was at work, Michael Kingerlee[13], (a former pupil), reports that:

> Don saw a group of boys climbing into the shut up Portman Chapel. He opened his window and fired his air rifle at the church bell which rang. After the second or third shot the pupils left much faster than they had climbed in, convinced it was the Portman ghost!

At one time, School attendance at Sunday church was obligatory. However, as Tim Nicholson[14] and others have commented, no one can remember seeing Don there. Although Don has always been a deeply spiritual person he has never been a church person.

Neither does it seem that he has ever had the desire to be an Assistant Housemaster. Mary describes his one venture in this direction, as 'a bit of a failure'. She relates the story of 'the boy who came along one night and poured out his love life to Don. He went on and on for ever and eventually Don said, "Jolly good, get on with!". As the boy, considerably cheered up, got to the door, he turned and said "His name is…."'

## The Old Stables Balcony

Some time after moving into the Old Stables, Don added a somewhat unusual extension to the flat. It was a cantilevered structure which hung over a considerable drop [51] which Mary estimates to have been 'about 17 - 20 feet up'. She remembers that Don got its weight-bearing capacity tested by, 'inviting the two largest people he knew to come and have tea on it. After this, the children were allowed on!'

[50] Portman Chapel, Bryanston

[51] Don's home-built balcony at the Old Stables

Richard Bawden, a pupil at that time, says that to make the balcony:

> Don cut down two tall straight fir trees and set them, when trimmed, into the side of the building at an angle to support a large balcony on which [he and others] sometimes, when invited after evening church in the summer, sat and had cider.

Eventually, Mike Dodd[15] (a former pupil), said the balcony became rather 'green, licheny and rickety and so was taken down'.

Although Don never became a true House Master, many pupils, including Brinsley Tyrrell, remember their visits to the Old Stables when Don was living there with his family:

> the privilege of going to dinner with Don, his wife Mary and their son and daughter. Having the best soup I have ever tasted served in wood ash glazed bowls. I was so nervous and Mary was so charming, I always looked forward to this.

[52] Photograph of a young Julian

[53] Don, Mary and Anne, aged about six months

Russell Polden,[16] another former pupil, also remembers:

> going up the stairs of the Old Stables, past various carvings, some of them suspended on string so they moved with the wind and sitting down to tea amongst other sculptures, some carved by Don, some by the boys. He always wore a smock and if he wasn't holding a mallet and a chisel, he was covered in clay or a bit red in the face after firing the kiln.

# Marriage and Children

The Old Stables was to be Don and Mary's home for nearly twenty years. It was here, as Don has written, 'that one of the best things that ever happened to [him] occurred....I married Mary.' (Anne their daughter, has described Mary as 'the wind beneath his wings'). This was in 1945, and today, Don recalls the years with Mary and his family at the Old Stables, as 'years…full of happiness'. However, they were not necessarily years of domestic comfort: for example, to begin with they only had a cold water supply with an old fashioned copper in the bathroom. This Mary 'used for washing nappies along with a hand-wringer over the bath'. However, they were amongst the first in their group of friends to own a washing machine. Eventually they had hot water when a Bryanston School Governor, Lord Verulam, put Rayburns into various Bryanston school properties. In 1947, their daughter, Anne [53] was born, then in 1952, their son, Julian [52]. Both, in Don's words, 'grew up in the special atmosphere and community of Bryanston.'

Mary was born (1920) in Rochford, Kent. She never knew her parents and thus spent her childhood years either in childrens' or foster homes. After such a sad beginning to life, all worked out well in the end. However, as Mary recalls, their honeymoon was not quite the most romantic of affairs! It was still war-time and they had no money, so they camped for a week in one of the fields belonging to Arthur Hickson, the Head of Oldfield School. Mary remembers walking along the front at Swanage and being told that the Americans had just dropped an atomic bomb. Not sleeping very well on the hard ground, she admits she could not wait to get back to their new home. However, once there, she had to instantly turn around and depart again. As a qualified nurse (having trained at the Radcliffe Infirmary in Oxford), she had been assigned to Southampton Hospital. After the War she continued nursing for a while at Blandford Hospital.

# Don: a spiritual man

From an early age, Anne has always shared Don's interest in metaphysics, philosophy and spiritual matters, particularly those associated with Eastern religions. During his life, Don has read widely in this area. Today, he reads the words of Sathya Sai Baba with his teaching of 'Love all - serve all'. Anne has written:

> He is a very spiritual man and the same energy that flows into his creativity also fuels an intense search to understand life's higher truths. We used to spend a lot of time sitting in his studio talking about spiritual and esoteric thought. He never minded his work being interrupted. He was a prodigious reader on these subjects and he usually requested books from me for birthdays and Christmas. It is a very important central part of who he is. Both my parents went out to India to an Ashram in 1993 when dad was 91 and again in 1994. He learned transcendental meditation in the 1960s and has practised it twice daily since then. I'm sure that this has been a large contributory factor in his longevity.

A selection of authors whom Don has read include: Alice Bailey, Guergieff, Paul Solomon, Maurice Nichols, Huxley, Julian and George Trevelyan, Krishnamurti, Jung and Ouspenski.

# Anne: early memories

As a father, Anne remembers Don as being 'a very happy, loving kind of man'; she never remembers a cross word. However, he was quite a 'poseur' (in the nicest possible way) as regards clothes! The following is part of an account of Anne's early memories of home life at Bryanston. (Other edited parts appear elsewhere in the book).

### Memories of Dad - Don Potter

> My earliest memories are of him wearing faded olive corduroy trousers and jackets. It was always very comforting and felt nice as a child. His clothing was different to what most people wore then. He worked in smocks, sometimes beige, sometimes striped with a red spotted handkerchief knotted over his head to protect his hair from the stone dust. I think he also wore work hats made from paper like Eric Gill. He used to make his own leather sandals and belts with homemade brass buckles. He still has a pair.

He carved little buttons for my coat as a child and made me a wooden jointed doll to play with. He used to wear a magnificent belted bearskin fur coat in the 1950's that was completely unique in that era and which he eventually swapped for a long fur-lined pigskin trench coat in the 60's. His shirts, always in dark rich colours, were embroidered on the front and cuffs by his sister Norah with traditional designs like the Dorset Woodman's smocking. Somewhere down the line he started to wear his uniform charcoal trousers, black shoes [the same design for as long as I can remember] and usually a charcoal or black pullover. The velvet wine coloured jacket comes out for special events!

His hair was unusually long for that time and was often the cause of some misunderstanding! He would occasionally return from shopping and say 'I think that it's time that I had my hair cut, I was called Madam in a shop today!' Another time a woman's car broke down in the village late one evening and she asked to use our phone. My father, standing there in his boldly striped men's pyjamas heard her say 'there's a nice lady here who's letting me use her phone!' He brushes his hair 100 times in the morning and always harboured a wish to have one gold earring like a pirate but never achieved this. This might have been due to the fact that although he has pierced several women's ears [at their request] with a needle and a cork perhaps he couldn't face doing his own! I'm told that I was a difficult baby who cried a lot and that he had made a hole through the wall into my bedroom so that he could attach a string to my cradle to be able to rock it without getting out of bed. A visitor is reputed to have arrived one day to find him carving under the archway at the Stables whilst simultaneously rocking my cradle with his foot!

….They have always made homemade wine - damson, dandelion, elderflower, rice, rhubarb the list is endless and most were an acquired taste but dad still prefers & drinks his homemade wine aged 100! The flagons used to be arranged along the beam in his studio like an alchemist's laboratory with glass tubes bubbling and fermenting. Dad often felt that 'purely in the interests of research and high quality' he should get a ladder and a straw and test the brews!

[54] Elizabeth Muntz Photography: Don Potter

He bought a motorbike from a friend who taught him to ride it once around Hyde Park before he set off for Dorset. Later they had an old Morgan three-wheeler car, which I remember required a thump from one of his mallets to change gear! Until they bought a Mini in the 1960's their main means of transport was a series of Vespas.

There has always been [and continues to be] a constant stream of visitors to their home. Seen through a child's eyes they were a mix of rather colourful characters with interesting faces. Many of them were artist friends wearing rather eccentric or individual clothes; others were old boys or their parents. I remember being particularly fascinated by a man who arrived for the night with a leather bag with a python in it. My mother would always provide delicious homemade food.

Dad used to grow sweet corn and tomatoes at the Stables. During the war he was known to lean out of the windows and shoot rabbits that were foraging in the vegetables which my mother used to skin and cook. My first glimpse of dad in the mornings as a child at The Stables used to be of him sitting in front of the Rayburn making toast on the end of a metal toasting fork. He was always the family breakfast maker thus allowing him quiet time to meditate and, at one time, do yoga in the early morning before we got up. He brought the whole family breakfast in bed on Sunday mornings and cleaned all our shoes. The breakfast routine only stopped in his 100th year. He usually walked up to Bryanston to teach three times a day coming home for meals. He invariably walked whatever the weather.

He built the kiln in the bowels of the cellars at Bryanston. It exuded dusty dank smells and was an Aladdin's cave of pottery in all its stages from gloopy clay mixing machines to the fine finished articles of his pupils. I remember the excitement created by the ritual of the all night stoking of the kiln while it was being fired and the magic of peeping into the chambers before it was unpacked to see the transformation that had taken place during the night

He used to play the cello and eventually owned a very fine one. I have many memories of him after lunch in the sitting room playing Bach's unaccompanied cello sonatas and of him playing with other musicians at Bryanston. It bought him great pleasure. I don't know who taught him and under what circumstances he learned. He had played the cello with 100 cellists at the Albert Hall when he was a young man. Music was an important part of our lives and we used to attend most of the concerts at Bryanston where he would sit rolling up [and unrolling] the programme absentmindedly as he listened.

Another hobby of his was photography [54] I remember the excitement in the family when the second hand Rolleiflex camera was delivered and the subsequent torture of posing for photographs while he fiddled endlessly with exposure meters and lenses. He would develop and print them in the blacked out bathroom and taught me how to do so as well.

He was always ready, if asked, to give an opinion on my choice of clothes and horrified if I had a rare spot! When I attended my first pony-club ball at the approximate age of 12 he insisted that I put lipstick and blue eye shadow on my face and debated whether he should fix sequins to my eyelids. While my friends were surreptitiously applying lipstick forbidden by their parents, I hurriedly wiped mine off when I left home.

He has a wonderful, if rather wet, sense of humour and is a great practical joker. He would happily rise to the bait of any joke played on him. Many is the time that Julian or I would pass him toothpaste instead of mustard at a meal or put holly in his bed at Christmas and he'd play along with it and act outraged. Our breakfasts in bed often contained a banana that he had filled with bread or empty upturned boiled eggs. He told us that he had once sent a letter to a friend with a note to the postman saying 'hey diddle diddle the stamps in the middle' to which the postman replied 'hey diddle day there's twopence to pay'!

He has a deep love of nature and has spent much time in the woods in and around Bryanston. He has a particular love of the three tall plane trees on the river path there. Dad seems to unconsciously touch furniture, pottery & natural fabrics as if his hands are 'reading' them in some subtle kinaesthetic way. I've noticed other potters and sculptors move their fingers over textures in a similar way almost as if they were reading Braille or experiencing the world through their hands.

He is physically strong and to date is still climbing ladders to clean out the gutters, chopping wood, cutting the village grass. He has fiercely resisted suggestions that he might like to relinquish some of his long held tasks. There is a certain vanity in his persistence and he believes that he is able to do what he has always done, whatever his age.

He has always loved my mother deeply and has relied on her to provide the practical structure of day-to-day life that has allowed him to devote his time to his work. This she has done superbly with great skill and modesty. For someone who came late to marriage and parenthood he has made an extraordinarily good job of both. Not only has he been unconditionally loving and supportive but he is in essence an extraordinarily kind, warm and courteous man. He has lived life on his own terms whilst being an inspiration to many people whose lives have touched his.

11 June 2002

Boarding at Sherborne Convent from the age of thirteen Anne did not come to know as many of her parents' friends as her brother, Julian. However, she did choose their friend, the sculptor, Elizabeth Muntz [55], to be her Godmother when she was christened at the age of thirteen.

Anne has written:

> Elizabeth was like a fairy godmother. She seemed to live in what seemed a magical environment for a child. Her home was filled with wonderful curiosities such as cups with birds on the handles, a big wooden painted apple that swung open to reveal cigarette, a painted Sicilian horse and cart and a glass diver in a bottle that went up and down when you applied pressure to the top of the bottle.

[55] Elizabeth Muntz letter-cutting in Anne's photograph collection.

## Julian: early memories

Julian was born in 1952 when Don was forty-nine years old. His earliest memories are of a father who seemed 'always busy working'. However, as Julian concedes, he did stop for elevenses, lunch, nap, tea time, then drinks at six! He also used to play Bach suites on his cello in his studio after lunch. Julian is also musical and plays the viola. With his cousin, Laurence Kennedy, his father, and sometimes others, he would play quintets and other chamber music. He would also regularly go with the family to concerts at the school. With many parents having strong connections with the Arts, Bryanston School was able to host concerts with performers such as Vladimir Ashkenazy, John Ogdon and Gervaise de Peyer.

However, as a child, Julian's parents' choice of holiday destinations rarely seemed attractive to him. He recalls: 'they always wanted to get to the remotest of all places - half-way up mountains, an island off the West Coast of Ireland, or Welsh cottages'. As at that time they did not have a car he remembers his father 'making two or three journeys on his Lambretta to the local train station with all their luggage'. Then, at the other end, they all had to 'get off a bus and walk miles to a cottage' in the middle of nowhere.

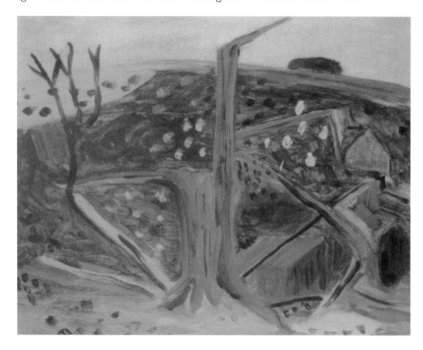

# Tony Twentyman

One treat for Julian, as far as cars were concerned, were visits from his honorary Godfather, the sculptor, Tony Twentyman [56].[17] This was because Twentyman would pick him up from school in his Porsche! Along with his brother, Richard Twentyman (who drove an Aston Martin), Tony had a love of racing cars. Julian remembers that Tony would stay quite regularly with his family, always bringing a bottle of gin. It was through an introduction from Tony to his brother, Richard, who was an architect, that Don won a series of church sculpture commissions in the Midlands (see page 159). Richard Twentyman was not only an excellent architect he was also a painter of landscapes in watercolour and oils [57]. He held a successful exhibition of his work in a London gallery in 1978.

Don first met Tony Twentyman in the 1920s when the latter came to a summer camp at the International Scoutmasters Training Centre at Gilwell Park in Essex. Twentyman was then a volunteer Scout Master for the 2nd Tettenhall Scout Group. At that time, as Don wrote for Twentyman's Retrospective (1990): I was working on various courses, and also searching for my soul as a self-taught woodcarver. There was quite a lot of my work around the place and this aroused Twentyman's interest'.

When World War II broke out, Twentyman joined the RAF but was captured at the Fall of Singapore and imprisoned by the Japanese for three and a half years. In his first letter (August 1945) of freedom, he wrote: 'I think I have also learnt a good deal about patience and tolerance and a better standard of values....'. On his return, he re-joined the family import-export business of Henry Rogers and Sons in Wolverhampton, but resigned in 1960 to become a full-time painter and sculptor.

In 1956, as Nick Arber writes, Don introduced Tony Twentyman 'to polyphant, a Cornish talc stone'. From then on Twentyman carved almost exclusively in stone, 'particularly in English stones, whose quarries he loved to discover and names to use in the titles of his sculptures'.[18]

Like Don, he was put up for an Associate Fellowship of the Royal Society of British Sculptors, being finally elected in 1983. At Dudmaston House, he created sculptures for the gardens of Sir George Labouchère who was both a friend and neighbour. Labouchère also commissioned Don to do some inscriptions for him (see page 172). Mary remembers that whereas Sir George Labouchère 'loved contemporary art, his wife preferred classic, so they had this sort of gallery/museum with his and hers'.

[57] Painting by Richard Twentyman

# The Old Forge

For Don and Mary there eventually came a time when they realised they would have to leave the Old Stables as their flat was in dire need of repairs. Mary remembers:

> the stairs were collapsing, the ceiling was falling in and so forth.... neither the School, whose property it was, or we, felt able to put in the requisite money. It was just at this time that for once, Donald came down to the village to post a letter and saw The Old Forge. He thought he could do something with it. The School was then negotiating to turn it into garages.

Don and Mary were able to buy the Old Forge on a ninety-nine year lease. They then set about its restoration with some help from a builder. All the family moved in, as Don remembers,[19] except for 'Mittie, our cat, who refused to come to the village. She adopted Ronnie King, who lived halfway there, and although he did not like cats eventually he came to love her and was a wonderful master until she died.'

One appealing factor of the Old Forge as far as Don was concerned, was that he could have a studio which not only took in the full height of the house, but was also adjacent to his home. Anne remembers a constant background noise of hammering, of rhythmic tapping at the Old Forge, which was reassuring in its way. However, before the family could move in, there was much to do. The Old Forge was in an extremely basic state: for example, there were no proper floors or stairs. Both were to come from the Old Stables block.

As Mary remembers:

> Originally [they were] the horse partitions, painted green, from the Old Stables. However, they were made of Burmese teak. Don asked the Bursar if he could buy them and the Bursar's reply was: 'Would twenty pounds be too much?' Don split the wood - half for the sitting room floor and half for the kitchen.

Alan Shrimpton remembers Bob Kemball[20] helping Don to cut the wood out to make 'the gorgeous red-brown stairs and floor-boards'.

The internal doors to the sitting room and to the kitchen originally came from the servant's quarters in Portman House and the kitchen work surface, from a discarded school dining room table.

Don made most of the furniture for their new home: from the long kitchen table to door latches. Antony Penrose[21], a former pupil, has described Don as:

> the original tinker - a make do and mend specialist. Sometimes he would bring his own work into class and work beside us while we were doing our set pieces. I saw him build a teak dining table out of wood he had salvaged from the old Portman Stables. The surface was deeply indented with hoof marks, but by the time he had finished the table was flawless. I learned more from seeing that table go together than from doing my own work.

Anne recalls:

> as my parents were both creative and had little money to spare, they tended to make most things they needed. Indeed our home has always had a rich organic feel to it. Clothes were generally homemade. He made glass tables with metal legs, lamp stands, fire pokers, chairs, screens and their bed; which was made from unseasoned wood that sprouted leaves in the spring! My favourite things were a revolving cupboard rather like the modern carousel in cupboards but this one was built in to the wall and had shelves. We used to swing it round as fast as we could as children to find what we wanted. It was a favourite with all our friends. He also made a triangular drawer that swung out of the wall and an overhead revolving light.

Mary, who by now had considerable weaving skills, wove fine wool covers [58] and rugs. Two of her cream rugs still sit before the hearth in their sitting room. Together she and Don made a five foot high, hinged screen; the frame was cut from yew and the infill woven with raffia and young, soft-green bamboos. The screen still stands just inside their living room door, although the green of the bamboo has long since faded. Altogether, the house today is as aesthetically pleasing, warm and welcoming as one can believe it has always been. It fits William Morris's statement that in your house you should have nothing except what you know to be useful or believe to be beautiful.

# Mary's weaving

Mary first began weaving when she accompanied Don, during one school holiday, to Bishop Otter College, in Chichester. Don used to go to meetings which were associated with the Society for Education in Art. At these meetings there were potters, weavers, artists and crafts people. At one such meeting Mary met Ella McLeod, who was then Head of Weaving at Farnham. Mary became interested in the craft and on their return Don made her a beautiful yew floor loom. Besides weaving, Mary was also involved in many other related fabric crafts.

Felicity Aktas, (née Helfer)[22] has written:

> Mary's textiles deserve more than a passing mention; her income and participation must have been pretty important to the Potters for many years. She was a full-time teacher and occupied half of the big room under the Science Labs [the other half being sewing, run by Mrs Sayers], and was mostly extremely popular. There were six looms and four spinning wheels being worked simultaneously, and there was always a queue for the looms. Mary was a patient and really excellent teacher, and encouraged individual flair.

> Bryanston's policy was that the first year pupils must take a half-term of spinning and weaving, a half-term of sewing/embroidery, a half-term of metalwork, another of wood-work, another of sculpture and art, another of pottery. All of them…..boys and girls.

Mark Helfer, Felicity's father, remembers that:

> When the Duchess of Gloucester….produced an offspring, a woodworking boy created a cradle for presentation and Felicity spun and wove the coverlet, of new white lambs wool. The Duke annually presented a prize for the best craft work, and [his] son, Martin, won it one year for a super inlaid backgammon/chess table. The following year, under Mary's supervision, he excelled himself by spinning, dyeing and weaving seven yards of tweed which Rachel, [Helfer's wife] made into a glorious cloak that she still wears for special occasions.

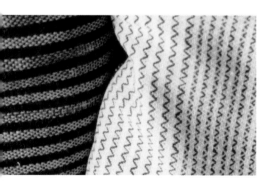

[ ] Mary's cushions: detail

[59] Back row, left to right Julian Potter, Cassandra, Iona, Mary, Don, Jude, Sophie, Toby
Front row, left to right: Julie Potter (Julian's wife), Kezia, Barry Singleton, Anne Singleton
(née Potter)
Photograph taken at The Old Forge, Bryanston on the day of Don's hundreth birthday,
21 April 2002

## Rural Dorset

Don's association with the county of Dorset began with his teaching appointment at Bryanston School. Dorset was still then a very rural county; a place where market towns and a few selected seaside resorts provided the biggest population centres. Through the 1940s and well into the 1950s, Dorset continued to be a county with relatively isolated communities and farms, which had become even more secluded as a result of war-time petrol rationing.

Amy Krauss, then a potter in Corfe [60], wrote of the local traffic situation in some letters to her friend, Joyce Scudamore:

> This village is very quiet now, lack of petrol makes a great difference to the traffic and it's much nicer than the days when you could hardly cross the road for the stream of traffic (1950).

Dependence on public transport was high:

> Two decker buses come through here (Corfe) to Swanage now and of course buses over the ferry - trains from Swanage are pretty often and only take 10 minutes and there is a bus stop (if you ask) nearly opposite the pottery' (1948).[1]

Krauss was to give Don his first pottery lessons at Corfe (see page 94), and for transport Don had to rely on his motorbike.

# Musical Interludes and Dorset Friends

Perhaps surprisingly, there was a fair scattering of artists, musicians and craftspeople in rural Dorset. Between the wars, landowners such as George Wingfield Digby[2] and Ralph Gardiner had two main interests: farming and the arts. Gardiner, who lived at Spring Head Estate, Fontmell Magna, was perhaps in advance of his time: he became involved in agricultural issues relating to the quality of soil and organic farming. Spencer Watson[3] talks of Gardiner's passion to 'revive a spirit, or maintain the spirit, that was in the British farm'. However, he also wished to revive 'village communities' and had a keenness for singing (including choral singing) and local dancing. He was closely involved with 'The Dorset Ladies' who started the County's Rural Music School.

Although most people now had radio in their homes, live music remained a major attraction. At Langton Matravers, between Corfe and Swanage, Hilda Spencer Watson, (Spencer Watson's mother), ran a theatre in buildings at Dunshay Manor [61]. William Scott, when a young artist, painted scenery for one of her productions, while Helen Muspratt[4], a studio photographer at Swanage, photographed stylised portraits of mother and daughter in Egyptian dance costumes. Over the years many well-known artists, musicians and writers came to Dunshay, including the psychoanalyst, Carl Gustav Jung. Many of the artists were friends of Mary's father, George Spencer Watson, who was a Royal Academician.

Don remembers going to various concerts and productions at Dunshay, and it was here, he believes, that he first met Mary Spencer Watson. It was also through attending local concerts that Don came to know the tenor, David Brynley (who had made his debut in the Beggar's Opera at The Lyric, Hammersmith) and the baritone, Norman Notley [62, 63].

[61] Dunshay Manor

[62] *David Brynley Norman Notley*
Pencil drawing by Elsie Barling
David Brynley on right

[63] David Brynley (right) and Norman Notley (left) at their Dorset home, Woolgarston

[64] David Brynley with former owners of Woolgarston, Mr & Mrs Bardell

# David Brynley and Norman Notley

Both Brynley (1902-1981) and Notley (1890-1980) sang in a sextet for un-accompanied mixed voices known as 'The English Singers'. The group was initially managed by the famous tenor, Stuart Wilson. In 1932 they re-named themselves: 'The New English Singers' and Cuthbert Kelly, who had become a Dorset-based musician, joined the group. As Spencer Watson recalls:

> They researched early English music and performed it round the table. They travelled to America, Japan and all round Europe… Norman set up home [with David Brynley] in this little cottage called Cotpot at Little Woolgarston [64]. They built a lovely barn studio for a music studio, for doing practices, still there now… Cuthbert Kelly (bass singer) used to come and they would practise for their world tours….Kelly had a room in a farm house down on Poole harbour, the most wonderful spot. He had two grand pianos, each end of this great room……

# Don's Years of Music

During his many years at Bryanston, Don regularly played in quartets, chamber groups and orchestras. His only regret concerning the playing of the cello was his 'late start' (see page 6). Having studied with Herbert Walenn for some time, Don:

> managed to become a pupil of Livio Mannucci, who was the cellist in the Brosa Quartet for a long time, and is one of the best cellists in England. It is from Mannucci that [Don] bought his treasured Italian cello which is now to be heard all over Bryanston when he is practising. His low notes seem to shake the very foundations of the building.[5]

Haydn, Mozart, Beethoven and Schubert have always been amongst Don's favourite composers: 'I loved Schubert; played the Schubert Quintet...... lovely, lovely.' For Don, music has always been 'a necessity, not a relaxation'. For him, 'carving came naturally, but music [he] had to work for.' Although he played in many concerts, he was only late once. This happened when, already seated with other quartet members and ready to start, he realised he had left his glasses at home nearby. The audience waited politely while Don disappeared to retrieve them and then the performance commenced!

Spencer Watson particularly remembers Don's sensitive playing in one Dvorak Quartet, while Elizabeth Greenleaves[6] recently recalled the 'dreamlike quality of his playing in a concert in the Edwin Evans Room' (c1945). Besides playing at Bryanston, Don also played at Cranborne Chase School. This was Bryanston's 'sister' school at nearby Crichel. For a short period, the composer Harrison Birtwhistle (b1934), then a clarinettist and teacher, was Music Director at the school. It was here, Don believes, that Birtwhistle composed his first opera: *Punch and Judy* (1968). During rehearsals, Don remembers relentlessly teasing another cellist, Amy Allen. He would count bar-rests incorrectly, and occasionally would succeed in deceiving Allen into coming in early with the cello line - an error embarrassing for any musician, particularly for the Principal Cellist and the School cello teacher!

Christopher Wellington, a former pupil of Bryanston and now a member of the Rasumovsky String Quartet, remembers that such rehearsals, under John Stirling (who was on the Bryanston music staff from 1936-46), would always be 'lively and exciting, not infrequently punctuated by an outburst from Amy Allen: 'The cellos must be heard!''. Of Don's playing, Wellington[7] has written that it was 'full of life and filled with a joy'. He said:

Don usually addressed his cello with a flourish - fluency and a certain panache expressed his enjoyment in playing. However, he contained this style to play in notable performances of 'Dido and Aeneas' - a string quartet provided the instrumental texture, while the part of Dido was sung by Joanna Donat (a pupil) of Cranborne Chase School - an outstanding performance which reminded everyone that Purcell composed his masterpiece for a girls' school. Don could be seen setting off to rehearse at Crichel on his motorbike, hair blowing in the wind (no helmets in those days!) with the cello behind him attached by an optimistic leather strap!

As a pupil, Michael Gill remembers that on occasions he would find his teacher 'not potting, but playing his beloved cello in the cellars'. It was by hearing the 'strains of a Bach Partita' coming from that quarter, that he first discovered Don was a keen cellist. Don would also play Bach Suites in his studio at home. As far as Don was concerned, as he once explained to a young Alex Wengraf: 'there was no instrument that could sing closer to the human voice: [it was] the most humane instrument ever made'[8]

Don only retired from playing when he was eighty-two years of age. Some of the other players had moved away, and he decided he was doing too many things. Another problem was his encroaching deafness so he decided the time had come to retire; however, his love of music continues.

# Elizabeth Muntz

Don and Mary first came to know Elizabeth Muntz, a Canadian, when she came to teach art at Bryanston School. This was when the School was looking to replace Anthony Fry. Muntz became both a family friend and Godmother to the Potter's daughter, Anne.

Muntz lived at Chaldon Herring with André, a Frenchman. Not being married, they earned the disapproval of villagers. As Spencer Watson recalls: 'In those days you couldn't set up in a village with a friend, a man…..but they liked her very much, and him…. he was a lovely chap. I think in the end they did accept it.'

[65] Elizabeth Muntz at work on the
Head of Theodore Powys

Muntz's cottage was called 'Apple Tree'. Mary (Potter) has described the
cottage as originally being 'two cottages knocked into one, with a long garden
and then the barn known as 'Ship's Timbers' at the bottom'. Muntz also had
two tiny cottages next door which she used to let students stay in when they
were with her.

Chaldon is still a small Dorset hamlet which is particularly known for its
literary associations with Sylvia Townsend Warner and the Powys brothers.
Muntz carved the head of Theodore Powys[9] [65] and also a stone inscription
to mark the spot where Llewelyn Powys' ashes were scattered (this is on the
Dorset Downs between Chideock and the sea).

As a sculptor, Spencer Watson rates Muntz as 'a very, very good portraitist.
This head of Powys…it's sculptural…..sound. She was clever.' However, Muntz
seemed rarely to engage with the freer, more interpretative dimension of
sculpture. Spencer Watson says:

[66] *Woman with Book*, Ash c1940 Mary Spencer Watson

She couldn't understand my sculpture with its hard edges. She used to say it was like two reliefs stuck together. I had been a pupil of Zadkine and loved hard edges [66]. But she.....with Dobson, it was all round.....all your form had to go round. She didn't like a form to stop with a hard edge. She worked with local stone and was a good portraitist of people and children.

Muntz, whom Don and Mary have described as a very warm person, loved children. Mary Potter, however, believes she would have been the most awful mother, even though she was a wonderful Godmother. In her memories of Muntz Mary's daughter, Anne, has written:[10]

I stayed with Elizabeth several times. My father would drive me over to Chaldon Herring on the back of his scooter and more than once she would meet us a few miles away from Apple Tree Cottage in her pony and carriage. You could hear the brasses ringing and jangling and the horses' hooves from quite a way off. I would climb into the carriage and go back with her to her cottage. Rumple her dog would always accompany her.

The animals were part of her and André's routine. I would be woken in the morning by hearing her open the front door. Rumple would rush barking into the garden and run around in the dew making fresh tracks and smelling the morning scents. In the evening I would help André mix up the special bran for John Barleycorn in the end room of the cottage. We would then walk down to his field, over the ford to feed him and bed him down for the night.

Out in the garden were endless treats to delight all imaginative children. A small turreted dolls house with china figures in which there was a secret passage from the house into the turret where a pirate with a parrot lived!

I used to play on her pond with a beautiful masted wooden boat endlessly loading and off loading cargo into its hold. In the middle of the pond stood a figure of a child carved by her. Stabled in her garden shed was a beautiful wooden rocking horse also equipped with brass bells and a silver hunting horn that we all rode on (I have that still).

[67] Anne outside the Wendy House at Apple Tree cottage

At the other side of the garden she had built a thatched Wendy House [67] situated in its own garden. Inside it was filled with Victorian dolls and furniture. It had proper glass windows that opened and at the back a stable for the Victorian horse and cow on wheels. I spent hours absorbed in play here. At Christmas time this was turned into a nativity scene and the village children used to visit it and, I believe, sing carols there.

Elizabeth had a remarkable ability to step into the mind of a child. When I went to stay with her she had always carefully selected books to put by the bedside such as E E Nesbit and Arthur Ransome. The biggest treat was a tin full of biscuits just in case one felt a little peckish during the night. Such treats were unheard of at home!

[68] Apple Tree Cottage, East Chaldon, 1950s Hope (left) and Elizabeth Muntz (right)

She had a woman who came in the morning and cooked a meal for André and herself and left it ready to be heated up in the evening. I don't think she was very domesticated. Her father had been the Governor of Bermuda when she was a girl. She had a portrait of herself painted as a child on her wall. The bookcases contained many interesting books such as *The Golden Bough* and a book written by her sister Hope [68].[11]

At Christmas time it was *her* presents that always created the greatest sense of anticipation and excitement as they were always so different. A beautiful little box with a black lead cat inside for good luck, a seal with a rose on to stamp my letters, a beautiful silver bracelet, a bottle from Venice and my two favourites: a tiny necklace of two fishes made in gold and covered in turquoise and purple kingfisher feathers with a letter explaining that it had been given to her mother by a sailor who had come from China with it. Her mother had given it to her and told her to give it to a little girl whom she loved as much when she was grown up. The other was a tiny walnut with a gold thread tie that when opened was lined in blue velvet and contained a china figure of the Virgin Mary and child.

I never felt entirely comfortable with Elizabeth (Muntz) as a child, partly because I was not good at being away from home but I feel that paradoxically whilst being able to create an extraordinary magical environment for a child to lose herself in she was not quite so adept at creating an emotional closeness with them. I last saw her when I was about 16 and have often wished that I could have known her in my adult years when I might have had a different sort of relationship with her.

## Mary Jewels

For a while, Muntz worked as an assistant to the sculptor, Frank Dobson. Dobson was married to Cordelia; the sister of the painter, Mary Jewels (1886-1977). It was through this thread of connection that Don and Mary came to meet Mary Jewels. Peter Tregurtha, Cordelia's son, remembers Muntz giving him 'a hammer with his name, Peter, carved on the haft, to try his hand in shaping stone'.[12]

Julian and Anne remember visiting Jewels with their parents. Don and Mary made several visits to Jewels' home: Vine Cottage in Newlyn, Cornwall. They bought one of her oil paintings, *Newlyn Harbour* [69], paying for it by instalments of £5 a month. Tregurtha says that *Newlyn Harbour* 'is typical of Aunt Mary's 'perspective', ships climbing slopes'.[13] Mary (Potter) said Jewels would write to them after receiving each payment, saying: 'thank you for the cheque; don't forget you owe me so much.' Marion Wybrow, in *The Innocent Eye*,[14] reports that the painter, Adrian Ryan, also bought paintings in a similar manner, as Jewels liked this particular kind of financial arrangement.

Mary Jewels never received any tuition in painting, but in 1919, Cedric Morris, the painter, handed her canvas, brush and paints and told her to paint. Her thick textured, unmixed oils have a direct and appealing quality; they have an immediacy that brings with them the smells and sounds of the sea: of fishermen, boats and harbours. However, she disliked anyone describing her work as naïve; or likening it to the work of the Cornish painter, Alfred Wallace. Peter Tregurtha, said that although his aunt never travelled, his mother, Cordelia did: 'Delia, as she was known [said that] the blue of Capri couldn't beat the blue of their Cornish sea.'[15]

[69] *Newlyn Harbour,* oil Mary Jewels

# Mary Spencer Watson

[70] Mary Spencer Watson 2002

Muntz became an Honorary Freeman of the Ancient Order of Purbeck Marblers, as did Mary Spencer Watson [70, 71]. These two sculptors became very close friends although Muntz was of an older generation. Spencer Watson remembers their first meeting:

> [We had] been told by Elsie Barling and Amy Krauss that there was a sculptor living up at Chaldon Herring called Muntz whom we must meet. With this in the back of our minds, my mother and I did a tiny little tour with our two horses and a pack horse carrying the tent and all the cooking stuff… we got to Lulworth and decided to camp…….we got permission from the farmer……there was a lovely valley going down towards Chaldon. Anyway, we were sitting in our tent, early morning, the horses were grazing round and a rider came by on a cob and who should it be but Elizabeth Muntz. That was the beginning of a very long friendship.

There has been an equally long friendship between Spencer Watson and Don and Mary Potter. They came to really know one another when Spencer Watson began teaching sculpture at Clayesmoor School, Iwerne Minster, in 1942.

During the first years of World War II, Spencer Watson ran Dunshay Manor as a dairy farm. She says that her family were quite insistent that she should not get a war job away. However, after about two years of very hard work, Mary's mother said Mary was becoming 'quite impossible' and suggested she wrote to various headmasters 'of the big schools around to see if she could get a job'. She succeeded, becoming artist in residence at Clayesmoor School. She taught four days a week, staying three nights at the school. They gave her:

> A studio, a big greenhouse, very cold in winter, but otherwise all right. I had the mornings to myself, except for the last two periods, and then the boys used to come in for their lesson and also in their hobbies period. It was a small model of Bryanston. It was during this time that I met Don. I was the opposite number to what he was doing, sculpture wise.

[71] *Standard Bearer* Purbeck Stone, 1990
Mary Spencer Watson

Teaching was never Spencer Watson's favourite activity:' I hated teaching. I just had to hold my hands behind my back, see them mutilating stone and it just didn't interest me at all. At that time half my mind was running the farm.' However, one advantage of teaching was that she was given some petrol coupons. This gave her the opportunity to:

> call in on Don on my way home. It was all quite fleeting, it was rushing from Clayesmoor back to the farm, but taking in a bit of fun on the way back to see this marvellous craftsman. I remember being very impressed with his furniture, he made his own furniture at that stage, and everything was touched with this magic crafts touch - and Mary, of course, and very little children. But I'm not awfully one for children ......I wanted to talk to Don.

It was after World War II ended that Bryanston opened a sister school at Crichel called Cranborne Chase School. Its first Head was Miss Galton, who had originally taught Mathematics at Bryanston School. Spencer Watson began teaching at the girls' school in about 1948 and was there for several years. She remembers:

> all sorts of celebrities' daughters [including] Elizabeth Whittaker, who became a sculptor and Mary Moore, the daughter of Henry Moore. After the War, the local councils began to build schools and they would employ a cheap, young, sculptor to do something in their school. This was a wonderful chance for me because I had always wanted to do sculpture with architecture.

Warmsley Lewis, an architect in Weymouth and friend of her mother's, gave her introductions and she took portfolios round various London architects. They gave her commissions:

> there was Frederick Gibbard, responsible for Harlow New Town; Easton Robertson, an old firm, mostly in Cambridge and Edgebaston; and in the inner city, St. Bartholomew's Hostel for Women....... I didn't have time for teaching.

It was about the same time, in the Fifties, that Don began a successful association with an architectural practice run by Richard (Dick) Twentyman. The firm was based in the Midlands and today still practices as Twentyman, Percy & Partners[16]. Don, however, was never in a position to give up teaching; he thus continued a dual career as both sculptor and teacher.

# Elsie Barling

Through various events and activities at Dunshay Manor and Corfe, Don came to meet what Spencer Watson has described as 'a coterie of crafts people and painters'. Amongst their number was the painter, Elsie Barling [73], who visited Don and Mary at Bryanston, in her 'old black car'. Always when the time came for her to leave, she would ask Don to reverse the car for her: somehow she never managed to master that mechanical manoeuvre.

Barling drew and painted extensively in Dorset [72]. She had a Retrospective at Dorset County Museum in 1977. Tim Nicholson has said that at one time, she taught John Craxton. She had a strong drawing hand and Dorset Museum has a collection of her drawings. These include two of her friend, the painter Frances Hodgkins [74], and others of David Brynley and Norman Notley [62].

[72] *Lulworth Cove* Elsie Barling

[73] Elsie Barling photographed at the time of her exhibition at Dorset County Museum, Dorchester, 1977

[74] *Frances Hodgkins* (in repose) Pencil drawing by Elsie Barling (1940s)

# Frances Hodgkins

It was not until her final years that Frances Hodgkins [75] achieved wide recognition for her painting. It was probably Amy Krauss who first invited Hodgkins to come and work in Corfe. The years there were to be Hodgkins' final years of life and work (1940-47). They were also years in which, as Myfanwy Evans[17] wrote, Hodgkins fell in love with Dorset: 'overcome by the beauties of its changing light, by the delicacy and depth of its colour, and by the strength of its unemphatic form. She said finally that it [was] the only place to paint.' Her subjects were local farms, fishermen's huts, the Purbeck coast, and the buildings and courtyards of Corfe.

In Corfe, Spencer Watson remembers:

> she would be seen around with a hat stuck on her head, a lot of fluffy hair sticking out, a smallish, stocky woman with a lovely sense of humour. Like her paintings a vision beyond other people's all the time, in her conversation and so forth……..it was always just, got that little edge to it, you went away and mulled over it.

Don and Mary knew Hodgkins through Elsie Barling and Kitty West (Katharine Church, the painter). West ran The Hambledon Gallery in Blandford. Mary Potter recalls that West would give Hodgkins presents of fresh eggs when she and Barling came to visit her. Hodgkins had known West and her husband, Anthony, for some years. In one letter she referred to them as: '2 delightful Dears Anthony & Kitty'.[18] Although Hodgkins' paintings were now selling for large sums of money in London, it was noted by her friends that she was personally reaping little financial benefit from such sales.

When Hodgkins first came to Corfe, Francis Newbery (founder of the Glasgow School of Art) let her work in his studio, but according to Spencer Watson:

> It was a cold, damp place. She used to lodge at the Greyhound, a very nice inn keeper there used to look after her a bit. She had all her meals there, but this awful cold [studio], not even an oil stove….a vast, old chapel, it was absolutely wicked, and all Fra's canvasses hanging around everywhere. How she worked there I just don't know. She went slightly off the top, it was the awful, awful, conditions. She was elderly and frail. She died at Herrison Hospital (a mental hospital). Everything was against her but she was a fighter, amazingly courageous. I met her several times but I was so much in awe of her, I was so very, very shy so I didn't really get anywhere.

[75] Frances Hodgkins with David Bryndley at Corfe

# Katharine Church (Kitty West)

[76] *Julian Potter,* oil 1954 Katharine Church

Katharine Church (1910-1999) was a very close friend of Don and Mary's. They first knew her in 1946, when she came to live at Tarrant Hinton with her husband, the painter and writer, Anthony West. For a while, Kitty taught life drawing classes at Cranborne Chase School, one evening a week. She also used to come over to the Da Vinci Society at Bryanston; this was an after-school activity ostensibly for the benefit of the boys. Kitty's and Anthony's son, Edmund, was then a pupil at Bryanston School.

During the war years, Church painted her first portraits of evacuee children. This subsequently led her to paint her own children, Edmund and Caroline, and the children of neighbours, friends and relatives, including a portrait oil of Julian Potter [76]. Much later in life, she phoned Julian to ask him to sit for a portrait drawing, which he did. She then put it in a silver frame and gave it to Don and Mary for their Silver Wedding Anniversary. When Don was eighty she gave him a watercolour of sunflowers. Continuing this birthday 'tradition', West's daughter, Caroline Duah, will be presenting a watercolour of *Portland Quarry* [77] to Don in celebration of his 100th birthday and his Retrospective Exhibition at Dorset County Museum, Dorchester.[19]

[77] *Portland Quarry,* watercolour, Katharine Church

[78] *Self Portrait,* oil, 1994 Katharine Church,

Under the name of Katharine Church, Kitty West exhibited at The Royal Society of Portrait Painters and the Tate Gallery. Having been a student at the Royal Academy Schools and then at the Slade, she was subsequently successful in launching herself as a painter. She exhibited with the New English Art Club and The Royal Academy. Ivon Hitchins admired and supported her work, while John Piper, during her visits to his home at Fawley Bottom, in Oxfordshire, encouraged her to have faith in her work, recognising in her 'a real painter' [78].

West was also close friends with the poet, John Betjeman and with Ralph and Frances Partridge. In Frances Partridge's *Diaries 1972-1975*[20] there are many references to Kitty West, as well as to other friends who were members of the Bloomsbury Group. Nearer to home, at Cranborne, West was also friends with Kit and E.Q. Nicholson (Kit was the brother of Ben Nicholson). Together they went on holiday to Varengeville in 1938, where West completed several collage works and watercolours.

Sometimes, Church painted with Hodgkins. They would go on a local trip to a nearby place such as Tisbury, where, for example, they both painted the farm buildings of Quarry Farm at Chicksgrove. Hodgkins also painted a large watercolour portrait of *Katharine Church* and a double oil portrait of her and her husband, Anthony.

As the owner of The Hambledon Gallery in Blandford, Kitty West was well known locally. She found running the gallery to be a successful but time-consuming business. She reflected afterwards that perhaps she should not have stayed with it so long, as it meant she had had too little time for painting. However, she held many prestigious shows at the Gallery, and for a while, Mary (Potter) helped her there.

## Mary Fedden; The Lion Story

Besides showing the work of Hodgkins and Piper, Kitty West also exhibited the work of college peers and friends such as Mary Fedden and Julian Trevelyan. Fedden has written about her visits to Kitty West and has also recently recalled a curious story of vanishing lions.[21]

We stayed with Kitty often as our son (Philip) was at Bryanston and we took picnics to the coast and drew around Portland Bill and all over the county. [Once] Julian, Kitty and Kitty's son (Edmund) and I were walking on Bulbarrow and as we reached the top there were two lions lying a few yards away. They looked at us for at least a minute and then slowly turned and walked away - then ran and jumped a stone wall and disappeared. We went down to Childe Oakford where we had a friend. We rang the police who didn't believe us and we never discovered anything about them. Very strange.

Mary (Potter) has said 'Kitty told me there was no two ways about it…it was a lion's tail that whisked over the wall…it was at the top of Turnworth Hill. It's lovely up there, lovely walks each side.'

Today, Fedden is a Royal Academician and as Mel Gooding[22] writes: 'Colour and simplicity [are] the compositional keynotes of her painting'. *Pansies in a Landscape* [79] is an early Fedden painting, dating from the Fifties. The colours of this work are not the vibrant ones which one now perhaps associates with Fedden's painting. However, she was beginning to use flowers in a landscape, as a compositional device, very successfully in the late 1940s. The mood of this particular work is again more muted in comparison to later paintings; perhaps it reflected more sombre, recent world events.

[79] *Pansies in a Landscape* 1950's Mary Fedden

# Helen George and James Allardyce

Besides the painters whom Don and Mary met through The Hambledon Gallery and Bryanston, there were local talented artists such as Helen George and James Allardyce. James Allardyce taught Art and Woodwork at Clayesmore Preparatory School which was nearby. He lived in a cottage at Charlton Marshall near Blandford. He made four drawings of Julian (Potter) [80] which Don and Mary commissioned when they knew Allardyce to be short of money. Julian rates Allardyce to be 'a good and sensitive artist', who sadly spent much of his life 'in and out of mental hospital.'[23]

Another local painter was Helen George. There were six children in her family, three of whom (including Helen) became deaf. She travelled to America when she was about twenty-one to see if a surgeon could find a solution to her deafness, but none was found. She had, however, learned to lip read before completely losing her hearing. Julian still remembers a comment she once made during supper at their house. Although already 'stone deaf 'she said: 'What a quiet village it is'.

George painted perhaps the only oil portrait we have of Don [82]. Mary and Don also have a delightful watercolour of *Hens* [81] by George. The date of this work is unknown.

[80] *Julian,* Pencil drawing James Allardyce

[81] *Hens*, watercolour Helen George

[82] *Don*, oil Helen George

The Dorset of the Forties was thus, although a rural environment, not one completely devoid of art and music. In fact, in its fragmentary way, it had a rich substance and vitality about it that seems quite enviable. Don and Mary's initial network of music and artistic friends, from both within and outside Bryanston, were supportive in a number of ways. Indeed, on Don's appointment to Byanston School, he sought their advice as to whom he should contact to learn something about potting. The answer was Amy Krauss, the potter in Corfe.

# Amy Krauss: Don's first pottery teacher

When Don first accepted the teaching post at Bryanston School he knew pottery 'was going to be a bit of a problem' as he had never done any before. This did indeed prove to be the case when he was 'confronted with a class of 18 potters, in a small pottery room, all clamouring for instruction'.[1] On the advice of friends he went to see Amy Krauss [60], who was, in Spencer Watson's opinion: 'a rather fine potter' [83, 84].[2] Krauss had worked with William Fishley Holland at Fremington in North Devon.

Krauss, known as Kraussie to her friends, lived at Redlane Cottage in East Street, Corfe Castle. She was originally, as Spencer Watson recalls:

> in partnership with some people who ran a little pottery at Sandford, where the old clay factory was. They had a tea shop, that kind of thing. Amy was trying to work with these people but they weren't a patch on Amy and she left them. I think she must have come into a little money; she bought this old cow barn in Corfe and started her own pottery there, her own kiln. She did these absolutely lovely things. She was interested in the work of Katherine Pleydell-Bouverie. Amy was quite unique. She was visited one day by a man at her pottery in Corfe who wanted her to make a coffee set in black.....she was researching black ware and it was a coffee set for Lawrence of Arabia.

Pottery

[83, 84] Black slip bowls, earthenware, sgraffito design, Amy Krauss

In a letter to her friend, Joyce Scudamore, in 1948, Amy wrote about her pottery with its thatched roof:

> I am waiting for the thatcher to do my barn roof. The straw has arrived and these high winds are blowing it all over the place!! I have also had trouble with the kiln - I had it repaired and now it's behaving like a devil.'

# Winchcombe Pottery: Cardew and Finch

With a minimum of knowledge gleaned from Krauss, Don survived his pottery classes during his first term at Bryanston. However, as soon as the boys departed for their summer holidays, Don 'raced off to Winchcombe to work with Michael Cardew and Ray Finch'. Cardew, like Krauss, had had lessons with Fishley Holland; indeed it was Holland who gave him his first lessons in throwing.

Cardew originally bought the pottery at Winchcombe in 1926, and in the same year, Finch came to work with him as a young apprentice of twenty-two. Finch had just spent one year at the Central School in London with Dora Billington, an inspiring teacher. When Finch joined Cardew he said:

> I knew I was taking a gamble and that the Winchcombe business was precarious but it was what I wanted to do. However acceptable the use of hand-made pottery is today you have to realise it was quite unusual then.[3]

None of those who came to work at Winchcombe were interested in the highly finished art pottery which was then being produced by various makers. Cardew described it as 'terrible stuff…..generally brightly coloured, extremely well finished and very, very overworked'.[4]

Cardew had been Bernard Leach's first student at Leach's newly established pottery in St. Ives. Leach had only just returned from Japan (1920) bringing with him the Japanese potter, Shoji Hamada. With Hamada, Leach built the first Oriental climbing chimney[5] in Europe.

Cardew believed that Leach took him on as an apprentice because of Cardew's passionate interest in the English slipware tradition; a tradition which Leach was instrumental in reviving in Britain. Using slip, Leach and his followers trailed free-drawn lines or made bold gestural patterns on their ware. They also used the sgraffito technique of scratching through a layer of slip to show the different colour of the clay or body beneath. Wood glazes were 'allowed to fall on the ware from the fire in the kiln'[6] and the bottom of pots were left unglazed so they could be lifted easily off their support. Glaze colours, mostly made from vegetable and wood ash, were restricted by the greatest temperature attainable by the kilns. Pots produced by Leach and Cardew in this manner were imbued with a spontaneity and warmth that sharply contrasted with the hard, meticulous work of industrial potteries [85].

The publication of Leach's *A Potter's Book* also had a positive influence on both potters and the buying public, though the earth-coloured pots took a while to gain a following.

In 1926, Cardew left Leach to set up on his own. He rented a pottery at Winchcombe in Gloucestershire, where, until about 1931, he made 'the most genuine lead glazed slip-ware since the eighteenth-century tradition died'.[7] In 1939, he moved to Wenford Bridge, near Bodmin in Cornwall, leaving Ray Finch (his apprentice from 1936-1940), in charge at Winchcombe. Initially, Cardew had no intention of ending his connection with Winchcombe; he just wanted to start a second pottery in Cornwall. In 1942, though, he left England to work in Ghana at Achimota College on the Gold Coast and, in 1946, sold Winchcombe Pottery to Finch.

The years of World War II were a difficult time for Winchcombe: 1939 was a 'time of great unpredictability' with Cardew away, and Charles and Sidney Tustin (both Winchcombe apprentices) called up for Army service. This meant Finch had to work long hours with only the help of seventy-six year old Elijah Comfort. Further help did eventually come from potters who wished to train with Finch. Most came for short periods. One of these early apprentices was Don Potter, who informed Finch that having been offered a teaching post at Bryanston, he needed to know enough about pottery 'to keep ahead of the little buggers'. As Wheeler writes (1998): 'Keep ahead of them he did, inspiring many pupils, including two of today's highly respected potters, Richard Batterham and Mike Dodd.'[8] After Bryanston, Batterham went to work with Bernard Leach at St. Ives for a year, while Dodd, after reading medicine at Cambridge University, went to Hammersmith College of Art. This, however, was not a success, and Dodd left after a year to start his own pottery in Edburton, Sussex.

In a recent letter to the author, Finch has written[9] that he was able to teach Don 'the rudiments of 'throwing' and some general information about clay glazes, firing etc.'. In particular, he remembers Don as having 'had a remarkable gift for the quite difficult skill of shaping clay on the wheel and I was quite astonished how quickly he learnt. He was of course already a fully trained sculptor.' In potting, Finch always saw 'human skill as the most important ingredient in the mix', although 'good clay, with a good body', was also very important: 'if you got a good body you could fit a glaze: it was easier to change the glazes than it was the body' [86].[10]

[85] *Cider Jug,* black slip with incised decoration through the slip, Michael Cardew

Instinctively, as Michael Gill has pointed out, Don felt 'closer to the earthy robustness, the craft potter' of Cardew and Finch, than to the 'more self-conscious work of Leach'. However, all these potters shared a common attitude to craft. It was, as David Whiting[1] has written, to do with Bernard Leach's belief: 'that the 'continuity in the potter's art depends on the "slow bodily transference" of ways of making things, from one pair of hands to another and from one generation to the next'.

Don has always felt a debt to both Finch and Cardew for allowing him to go to Winchcombe whenever he was free during school holidays. Richard Bawden, believes it was his mother, Charlotte Epton (potter and founder of Denman College in Oxfordshire), who first suggested to Don that he went to Winchcombe. She knew Cardew and Finch, as she had worked at the Pottery from the mid to the late 1920s.

[87] Mixed wood ash glazed pot,, stoneware, 28cms (11") top diameter Don Potter

# A good eye for form

In the preface to Cardew's *Pioneer Pottery* (1969),[12] Bernard Leach wrote that Cardew possessed the potter's prime gift: a sense of form. This sense of form, an almost 'intuitive' knowledge, was something which Don possessed in good measure [87]. He was also able to communicate this 'sense of form' to his pupils. One former pupil, Richard Batterham, is now recognised as 'one of the few throwers who works really well on a large scale'. Even as a pupil at Bryanston School, he was tackling large size pots [88]. Mike Dodd believes Batterham to be 'the most talented thrower we are going to see for a century'.

Without Don, Batterham says he would never have done pottery: 'He was special - he never directed anyone, he just tapped them into place.' Bawden, recalls:

> Don was not only a superb craftsman who showed you how to go about a job, but also how to see and appreciate form and the quality of materials used. He would discuss with you what constituted a good and strong form and point out with his hands and index finger where it was weak, and where there might need to be a change of direction. He would stand back and make you look.....the starting point was what you were doing. He did not....make one figurative or abstract.

Antony Penrose writes that he was always aware of Don's stature as a potter:

> and indeed, it always seemed to be the pottery where he was most at home, most relaxed and talkative. One day I recall I was with some boys standing around watching him working at the wheel. "What do all you lot want?" he asked in a gruff but kind sort of way. "We just like watching you work," a boy said. "Well, watching a good craftsman at work is a good way to learn," said Don, and then realising he had said something that might be construed as self-complimentary, he added quickly "and if you look around you might find one somewhere." Then he launched into an appreciation of Bernard Leach.

[88] Richard Batterham in the Pottery at Bryanston School

# The Pottery

Bryanston Pottery in the early Fifties, as described by Bawden, was: 'in a cellar below the main basement corridor, down a dark dusty spiral stone stair into a dimly lit cavern thick with powdered clay, cobwebs and even more dust'. Here, Kit Opie[13], a pupil over twenty years later, remembers Don could be found: 'like an alchemist, working in the bowels of the building with wheels turning, clay flying and kilns roaring'.

Whereas some pupils found it incomprehensible that a number of their peers put up with 'conditions like this', others, such as Stephen Spicer[14], who was potting under Don in the late Fifties, saw the pottery as a 'warm, convivial atmosphere' where 'a friendly dragon was kept…. in the shape of a two-chambered kiln, the warmth of whose breath could be felt all the way up the staircase walls, past many floors above'.

One of the youngest visitors to Bryanston pottery must have been Simon Warrack,[15] who subsequently became a pupil at Bryanston:

> The very first time I met Don I must have been 5 years old with my mother who had also known him since she was a baby having grown up in Bryanston village next door but one to Don and Mary. We went to meet him in the Pottery room which in those days was in a space deep in the bowels of the main school building, below the basement corridor. He was renowned at the time for having actually kicked a boy into one of the clay bins for some heinous crime, so I was a little nervous. He taught me, aged five, to throw a pot on a wheel and after some pretty messy trials we actually managed to produce a very small turned pot. My brother, aged three was also given some clay to model and he produced an abstract work which he proudly announced to be an ashtray.
>
> We had a wonderful afternoon but what really struck me was that a few days later Don turned up at our house in Durweston with the two objects which he had glazed and fired with all the care of a perfect pot; my father has them to this day on his desk. However, this really struck me as a five year old because he treated both me and my little brother like adults and taught us properly how to work the clay and then treated our results with the same respect as he would his own works. This is the greatest compliment when you are a child and I never forgot it.

# Building a Wood-fired Kiln

When Don first went to Bryanston there was a coal-fired kiln, but he found it very difficult to get hold of decent coal because of the War. Thus, when he returned from his first visit to Winchcombe (1941), in enthusiastic mode, he was more than happy to set about building a wood-burning kiln for firing earthenware. Michael Gill says that he used the design drawings of Mr. Baker, from the Rural Industries Bureau,[16] who wanted it built to see if it would work. The wood-kiln, as Bawden remembers, was about twelve feet in length and had two chambers, with a long entrance to accommodate long logs felled on the Bryanston Estate.

Both Gill [89] and Bawden were amongst Don's first pupils.

Gill relates that:

> Since Donald also ran the Sculptorium and the metal workshop he was able to set some of us pupils to work, shaping tapered arch firebricks while Peter Glover[17] made the metalwork supports for the kiln (see page 120).
>
> Every arch brick had to be tapered. It worked very well because there is nothing better than a tapered arch firebox for compressing the gases which get them hotter as they go into the tapered tunnel. The metal strapping was needed because as the kiln is repeatedly heated and cooled, it gets hotter, it expands. Unless there is something to push it back again when it cools, it will get bigger each time and finally fall apart.
>
> It was a combination of Don's Metal workshop and the Sculptorium which built the kiln and that took the first term that I was there although some of us did make beginners' attempts at throwing on the large industrial "Boy Wheel". This was a great big 8ft wooden wheel with a rope round it which goes down and round a pulley at the bottom of the wheel. It was a Stoke-on-Trent, Victorian production wheel, it was there in the Pottery when we started. (The boys later made some home-made kick wheels).

[89] *Jug* Earthenware, brush design with slip, height 12cm (5") Michael Gill. Made at Bryanston

# First Firings

Michael Gill also states that:

> The next term we had our first firings and the kiln performed very well - we were given special permission to get up at six o'clock in the morning to light it and it would get up to temperature sometime between 8 and 10 in the evening. We made a pyrometer in the Physics lab by using a small telescope in which we put a torch bulb. When you focussed the filament of the bulb and saw it against the unfocussed red through the spy-hole of the kiln you adjusted the current until the filament was invisible. You then read the temperature from the galvanometer, which we calibrated over several firings with cones.

> I remember one particular firing when we first tried out Fremington clay because that was the clay which Fishley Holland, the Devon potter, was then using. This was at a time when we had become interested in borax glazes and opalescence. We must have been a bit too enthusiastic because when we unpacked the kiln two days later there were no pots, only pools of very beautiful glazes on the shelves to show for most of a term's work!'

## Second Kiln for Stoneware

In about 1951, Don took down the earthenware kiln and built a new one for stoneware. Batterham later copied the design when he built his first kiln at Durweston (1959), although he 'made the mistake of thinking that if you have only one person you have it a twelfth of the size….it was a bit small!' Today he works with a similar kiln but it is fired by oil and much bigger! In the photograph, Batterham is packing the kiln as a young pupil at Bryanston with Derry Ormond [90].

Bawden remembers the day:

> when Don felt it was time we progressed from earthenware to stoneware he lugged a great oxygen cylinder from the metalwork department, and the temperature soared as never before. The heat was enormous. The chimney went up through the centre of the school and the staircase wall glowed!

A glowing school wall was not just a one-off occurrence, as one pupil, Philip Trevelyan[18] remembers:

> We were always hoping that his stoneware kiln firings would set fire to the school and on occasions, the school fire service was called on to cool down walls which had become extremely hot!

Sometimes, however, the School's vengeance must have seemed sweet. Brinsley Tyrrell remembers:

> Don in a foul mood all day. It's April 1st and he has been up on and off all night manning the school fire brigade (which he was in charge of) answering fire alarms even though he knew the calls would be April Fools.

Quin Hollick remembers 'going down late at night to see the progress of a firing when Don would be on vigil'. Sir Terence Conran [91] remembers that it was at such times Don would join them in a glass of beer.[19]

Hollick recalls that at:

> One time Don was experimenting with the oxidizing stage of the firing and was piping pure oxygen from a large cylinder. I think the firing was successful but he did manage to melt the iron grid in the fire chamber.

Penrose recalls that the wood-fired kiln:

> tapped into one of the vast chimneys which must have been 25 feet long, all home built out of refractory bricks and scrap iron. I recall looking through the peep hole at this terrifying white hot inferno, and watching while [Don] swung open a counterweighted hatch and dropped in another log. The heat coming off the brickwork rendered it nearly impossible to get near the thing. The extreme height of the chimney gave such a huge up-draught that the kiln roared away for the 36 hours or so that Don stayed in the basement patiently stoking and monitoring the progress.
>
> Today such a thing would be unthinkable. In this climate of risk-aversion people like Don are not allowed to build kilns, and so how do the young of today learn to improvise? How do they really learn the principles of how things work, and how to achieve things without wonderful facilities? I recently saw a brochure of the new craft centre at Bryanston. Spectacular, pristine and full of the latest gadgets, but not the sort of place where Don would teach his special magic.

[91] Pots made by Conran in the mid 1940s

# Clay

Don never bought ready-prepared materials, except for sand that had been ground-up to 200-sieve. In the Forties and Fifties there were few commercial suppliers, and those that existed, such as Wingers, supplied mostly to the commercial trade. In any case, starting with the 'raw stuff', Don worked on the Leach principle of 'work from the ground, upwards'. Once when Leach was asked, 'Why not use ready-mixed clay?' his answer was: 'Why begin at the end?'[20]

The clay they used when Batterham was there 'came from Corfe Mullen. We used to mix it up and dry it out in the boiler room. There was never enough. It came raw as dug and had to be mixed and sieved and so forth.'

Spicer remembers that:

> there was a clay mixer in a far room and a trough of plaster with a greenhouse heater underneath for drying the material. The quality of clay which Don took such trouble to prepare was very plastic and just rolled up like a carpet; it produced some of the finest pottery that could be seen anywhere, with a huge variety of ash glazes.

# Glazes

When Mr. Baker gave Don the kiln design, his only instruction concerning glazes, as Michael Gill records was:

> 'Oh you can make a glaze by mixing clay, red lead and sand.' That's essentially all we knew to start with. He also said: 'and you can make borax glazes too'. So we got some borax. I think he gave us a few possible combinations that we could try to start with. It was a very hit and miss business to start with, we really did learn by our mistakes. We tried everything we could think of.

Don also copied the method of grinding cobalt pigments from Leach's *A Potter's Book*. This took a very long time. As Gill comments: 'people in African countries did this for hours while they told stories to the people who worked decorating the pots'.

Don was always as excited as his pupils, when, as Kingerlee writes:

> the kiln was opened up to reveal some of the wonderful glazes that he had mixed for us to use on the pots. Some of these colours had been created by the wood gases and nobody could ever know if the fire had been stoked at the right time with oak logs, or perhaps we should have used more beech earlier, and what about that piece of ash that Don had insisted should go on next?

# Tree Felling

Pottery involved not only hours in the Pottery Room but also taking part in activities such as tree-felling and clearing on the estate. This came under the aegis of Pioneering and was an alternative option to Cadet Service-Training. Terence Conran[21] remembers that as a Pioneer himself, it was a:

> marvellous thing....... On two or three afternoons you could go off and learn forestry, build a Greek theatre or, as in my case, build a boathouse and begin work on an observatory.

Don was renowned for his quickness in getting out a chain-saw and mustering 'a gang' of helpers. Penrose recalls that Don 'collected and seasoned the logs years in advance so they were tinder dry'. Bonfire ash would also be gathered from any wood or scrub burning.

For Alan Shrimpton,

> one great pleasure on moving into Bryanston village, was to have Don as a near neighbour. Our closest working partnership saw us heading off into the woods with chainsaws and my VW workhorse. Len Taylor (School Woodman 1948-c85) let us collect fallen wood he had no time to deal with and we prided ourselves on our discrimination. Beech and Ash were tops, Sycamore, good, and the occasional Holm Oak; Elm and both Chestnuts were strictly for the fungi.

[92] Wood ash bowl, stoneware, conical ribbed bowl with brown oatmeal glaze c1970-80. Height 12.5cm (5") Pleydell-Bouverie

# Katherine Pleydell-Bouverie

According to Mike Dodd, an expert on glazes himself, Don has always had a good eye for glaze quality. He never researched glazes, but did keep a notebook of glaze recipes from other potters, particularly those of Katherine Pleydell-Bouverie (1895-1985), more familiarly known as 'Beano'. Pleydell-Bouverie dedicated sixty years to making ash-glaze pots in the Sung style [92].[22]

It was in the 1920s that Sung pots aroused interest from Leach and other potters in England. Gill remembers that Pleydell-Bouverie's 'house was wonderful.... a funny sort of mixture of being arty and at the same time quite Victorian. There were lovely great Sung pots, tall, elegant vases that she'd prop open doors with.'

Don used to take small groups of pupils to see Pleydell-Bouverie. In 1946 she had moved to Kilmington Manor, near Warminster in Wiltshire. Brinsley Tyrrell still clearly remembers: 'Don driving a group of us to visit Pleydell-Bouverie, a charming lady, and as I have since learnt a legendary potter. Her incredible tithe barn, her collection of priceless pots and the gradual realisation that Don held a privileged position in the elite of British Craftsmen.'

Pleydell-Bouverie must have known Don for some time before he accepted his post at Bryanston, because in a letter from William Rothenstein to Pleydell-Bouverie in 1934[23] Rothenstein wrote: 'Yr young wood-carver came to see me last week - he is certainly gifted & shd get on well'.

Pleydell-Bouverie first became interested in ash glazes when she spent a year (1924) at Bernard Leach's pottery in St. Ives. Norah Braden, Shoji Hamada and Tsuronosuke Matsubayashi were also there. From 'Matsu' in particular, she learned about clay, kilns, and glaze chemistry, about which she took meticulous notes. She invited 'Matsu' to her family's seventeenth-century estate at Coleshill in Berkshire in 1925, where she was then living. Matsu helped her construct a double-chamber wood-fired kiln next to the water mill.

In 1928, Norah Braden joined her. With her support for eight years, Pleydell-Bouverie carried out a systematic series of experiments into glazes, using the ash from a wide variety of trees and plants from the estate. She also, as Phil Rogers[24] (1991) writes: 'took advantage of a number of local clays including an ochre, which together with ball clays and china clay from Devon and Cornwall made up the several clay bodies that were used simultaneously'.

The texture and colour of many Pleydell-Bouverie glazes are quite beautiful. Muriel Rose[25] describes 'creamy matt-whites and light greys derived from grass and reed-ash, enhanced sometimes by a defined crackle; olive bronzy greens, dark browns and lighter greens from the ash of various trees; and a particularly beautiful quiet blue from the ash of laurustinus. These glazes were all made after the same formula: a measured quantity of ash, previously prepared by burning on a clean hearth, then washed and finely sieved, plus the same part of feldspar added to a half part of ball clay from Dorset.'

From an initial dual interest in chemistry and pottery, one of Don's pupils, Michael Gill, has maintained a life-long interest in glazes, conducting experiments with materials in Copenhagen, Helsinki, Johannesburg and other cities. Another pupil, Mike Dodd, has formulated glazes from naturally occurring materials local to his potteries in Sussex, Cumbria, Dorset and Somerset.

In a letter to Bernard Leach in 1930[26] Pleydell-Bouverie wrote: 'I want my pots to make people think, not of the Chinese, but of things like pebbles and shells and birds' eggs and the stones over which moss grows.' One can imagine Don feeling in sympathy with such descriptive images of pottery. A comment: 'Like black boot polish' indicated Pleydell-Bouverie being less than impressed by one result![27]

Batterham recalls that whenever they visited Pleydell-Bouverie, she was always welcoming; she even remembered their names. In later years, she also became 'a generous, constructive and supportive friend' to him. She was 'positive without being dogmatic. She had an incisive, commonsense mind together with a lovely, slightly impish, full-flowering smile and a wink.'

Once when Don, whom his family labels as 'a fidgeter', was having tea at Kilmington, he accidentally broke one of Pleydell-Bouverie's silver teaspoons in half. He was mortified, but a few days later a note arrived from Beano, saying he was not to worry about the spoon, it was of no consequence. Such kindness was much appreciated by Don.

In Pleydell-Bouverie's late years at Kilmington, she found the long firings too much for her and so, as Gill relates, 'she had an electric kiln in the barn and made little pots, trying her glaze experiments'. However, she felt she never succeeded in getting as good a result from the electric kiln, which she called a 'good servant' as from her wood-fired kiln, which she described as 'an inspired partner'.[28]

Dodd remembers one visit from school in particular:

> There was this famous cupboard under the stairs where she kept lots of pots, a bit like Bernard Leach's kitchen with a cupboard with lots of pots. But my first impression going into the house was a mantelpiece with Four Tang objects on it: a horse, a camel and a Samurai or whatever the equivalent in China.....wonderful. One pot I really remember coming out of that cupboard was a little, fluted bowl with what she called a hawthorn ash glaze on it; it was a fat, celadon, lovely, quiet bowl.
>
> Hawthorn ash - I've tried it several times, never come out like that, that's the only trouble. She is the woman on ash glazes, she tried everything from roses to laurel bushes to everything.
>
> Such visits were not particularly organised in Don's mind. I think he probably just took us there because she was a good potter and she lived locally. He just allowed Pleydell-Bouverie to take over. I doubt he even discussed with her what she was going to do. Pleydell-Bouverie's work has a sense of warmth and Don's has that too, wanting to hold, very tactile.

In the same tradition, Dodd's work also has that same warmth and tactility. He continues to experiment and invent new .variations of glazes, using 'a range of locally occurring rocks, clays and wood ashes to expand and deepen form'; his pots have, what Cardew called, 'that glow of life'.[29] It was from Don that Dodd learnt about the enriching qualities of wood ash glazes.

Ben Platts-Mills,[30] a former pupil, remembers one particular occasion in the Sixties, when they:

> burned only holly in one firing to have ash for a holly glaze - and walnut in another. What a beautiful thing to have been allowed to do in a life. We made the pots, burned the wood, he stayed up all night, we sieved the ash and glazed the pots and fired them to make things that most of us can only meet in a museum. What luxury it now all appears to have been.

# Don as Pottery teacher: Pupils exhibit at Heals

Michael Gill, along with another Bryanston pupil, Peter Barlow,[31] were amongst the first young people to exhibit their work at a Schools Pottery Exhibition at Heals, in Tottenham Court Road, London. In 1947, Harry Trethowan wrote a glowing review about the exhibition in *The Times Educational Supplement:*[32]

> There is a remarkable collection of pottery made under the direction of Donald Potter - himself a student of Eric Gill - by boys between the ages of 14 and 17 at Bryanston School, Dorset. Made of red clay, and with glazes of deep rich brown, cool terracotta and Chinese white, and other unusual colours, there are some pots worthy of a master craftsman.....the slip-ware too, has a definite personality without being laboured. The forms are simple, strong and natural......These students have impressed their work with an individuality which marks the good direction of the master while stressing their own understanding and appreciation.

Bawden's description of Don in the Pottery bears similarities to those who remember him in the Sculptorium, that is, a person who was:

[93] *Dish*, slip-trailed drawing of a head using manganese and white slips, 1961, Stephen Spicer

[94] *Eel plate*, slip-trailed drawing, c1950, Richard Batterham

physically strong, hair flowing back like Michael Heseltine. He would stride in, wearing an apron, cowboy shirt and dark corduroys. He was never deliberately unkind; however, if you were not interested, Don had no time for you. 'You', pointing with his finger, 'bugger off. I don't want anybody who's not prepared to work.'

Once, Warrack remembers Don chasing another pupil around the sculpture room with a hammer for swearing. 'I will not have anyone *** swearing in my *** workshop so get out and come back when you have learned some *** manners.'

In the late Fifties, Spicer said they:

> mostly (worked) on slip-decorated moulded dishes [93, 94]. Don's influence was absorbed by a kind of osmosis or suggestion as to what might be done and where my abilities lay. This joy and understanding of thinking through an extremely fecund material stayed with me past Art College...... You felt strongly that Don intuited a need in someone and participated in 'where they were at'.

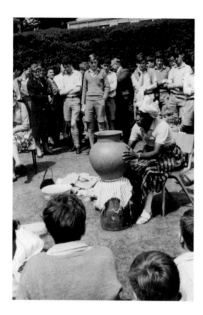

[95] Ladi Kwali at Bryanston, 1962[34]

With Don as teacher, Dodd remembers:

> there were no frilly edges, no false pretensions, it was an infusive sort of teaching because he was grounded himself in good method; good vision that was natural to him. It wasn't forced, he wasn't trying to impose .You weren't exactly taught - you were exposed to quality work.
>
> He used to put very good pots here, in the area of the kiln opening. I don't know whether this was intentional or not, maybe it was the only area that was free, I don't know, but he used to put the Cardews and the Bernard Leach pots here. I can remember unpacking this kiln and seeing a Cardew I hadn't seen there before. It was that pot that really woke me up to pottery, it was a Cardew pot, even though it took me another eight to ten years to really appreciate his work. He provided that environment to which you either responded or you didn't. If you did he then encouraged you further…you worked with him.
>
> It was all about the thing not the intellect. Once a student went up to Hamada and said 'Well what's so special about your work?' and he said 'Well, if you can't see it I can't tell you, and if you can see it, what's the point in me saying anything?…… and that's Don. I can remember my father trying to explain something to me verbally and I'd say 'Dad, don't explain it verbally, show me, then I'll remember it' and Don was like that.

What Don was able to give pupils, such as Rodney Lawrence.[33]

> was a very good grounding. One of the things I've always found helpful is ….I tend to do things in a fairly slap dash fashion after a while, I don't really notice what's going on and he started the fight against that side. He started telling you that there was a standard, it wasn't just, Oh! I can make this, it was how <u>well</u> could you make it?

He would 'show you what was possible and then give you a free rein'. In other words:

Don Potter: An inspiring century

You were taught craft which was a liberating experience. He had a superb eye.....He would encourage you if you clearly showed interest and ignore you if you didn't. He felt unless you were yourself encouraged by what you were doing, he couldn't do anything. He would introduce students to pottery by taking them to exhibitions, or to see Pleydell-Bouverie, to London or Primavera.....he sowed the seeds and if you responded, became interested through that sort of exposure, if he got your attention, he was good.

It was through Don's friendship with Michael Cardew that the celebrated Nigerian potter, Ladi Kwali, came to Bryanston in 1962 to give a demonstration of hand-built pottery [95]. It was from Cardew that Kwali learned how to use a potter's wheel which supplemented her own highly skilled hand-building techniques. Mary and Don remember her visit well.[35]

Lawrence, who went on to study studio pottery at Harrow School of Art, today makes both domestic stoneware and one-off decorated pots, the latter touched with the definite brush of humour (see page193).

Besides more confident pupils, Don also welcomed the inquisitive but shyer student to the pottery. One such visitor was John Richter,[36] who remembers that:

On arriving at Mr. Cowley's English double-period one early spring morning, each pupil was handed a slip of paper. It read: 'This person has permission to pursue whatever he is doing until the bell.....For me it was a fortunate chance to open the door by the Front hall and descend the dark stone stairs to the Pottery. As I nervously did so, there were loud sounds coming up. Then, before me, a long cavernous room with eight or so potters. They had rolled up sleeves and muddied aprons. Three or four were working kick-wheels, with lumps of brown earth rising into life; others were modelling, wedging, or decorating pots and there was Donald Potter in the middle of it all, talking, laughing, and tossing large logs into the already roaring kiln. The noise, the warmth and the smells were intoxicating. Within minutes (Don offered no challenge or surprise at this unexpected visit) I was kneading a lump of clay and had been assimilated into the noisy scene....I believe in that moment I saw him most completely in his element.

Raymond Wyatt,[37] another former pupil, has written that Don let people: 'discover themselves; to create, mould, form, throw, decorate and feel the materials [they] used'. In the *Saga* magazine (summer 1954) Don wrote of Wyatt:

> We do not talk much about self-expression, child art, significant form or creative living........There is a young lad who spends a lot of his spare time with us making the most charming decorated platters with quite an unconscious natural sense of design. His answer when I suggested he should do some work in the Art room was, but Sir, I have never liked Art!

Sometimes, as Platts-Mills remembers:

> Don's teaching method employed the Zen of manipulated disaster. How I hate Zen today. We did one of those divine firings with tenmoku celadon and those rare ash glazes and on opening the kiln found a scattering of bits of sand and fire cement all over the front pots.
>
> For a potter that will mean no bread, no jam, no tea today, but for us it was the luxury of learning, the experience of having destroyed such beauties while filling the gaps between the bricks in the door of the kiln with too much gusto. I remember DP. doing a short range lob with a flick of the wrist which helps cement stick to the bricks. And then we were all four of us chucking it.

Many, such as Spicer, found their time with Don to be:

> an excellent foil for academic subjects, psychologically, especially if there was a dragging sense of self-worth or ineptitude or lack of interest. All stages of a job (in potting) were equally deserving of your attention, including and especially clearing up, in case you thought other things were more worthy of your time.

Alex Wengraf says he still has 'a small glazed pot, made under Don's direction, broken now, and glued, a bit like an Olmec shard. It is my only artistic creation to have survived in existence, but it is enough'.

Some have returned to serious potting after a career in another profession: for example, at the beginning of the Seventies a fourteen year old Kit Opie went to Don's pottery classes for a year. They had been recommended by his uncle, David Canter,[38] who was both a past pupil of Don's and founder member of the Craftsmen Potters Association. In his reports Don wrote that Opie was ' a very enthusiastic boy….and 'seems to enjoy working with clay'. It took, as Opie writes: 'another thirty years' to find out how much he did 'enjoy working with clay'. Retiring from a career as an Economic Researcher he has now become a full-time potter, in the 'tradition of Leach, Batterham and Dodd'. Like many other ex-pupils, he is grateful to a teacher who instilled in him 'a love and appreciation for clay and pottery'.

## Yemeni pottery

For many of Don's pupils, the full effects of his inspiration and teaching did not surface until many years later. For example, it is because of him that the Department of Ethnography at the British Museum now have one hundred and eighty-one pieces of Yemeni pottery. It was as a Medical Officer for a British oil refinery in Aden that Mark Littlewood[39] first became captivated 'by the variety of shapes and decorations of the ware' that he saw in the market places. His first few buys turned into a large collection which he donated to the British Museum (details of which can be found in *Yemeni Pottery* by Sarah Posey).[40] The pottery ranges from domestic ware used for cooking, serving and storing food, to 'special use' objects, such as incense burners, water pots and preparation dishes.

In a preface to *Yemeni Pottery*, Littlewood writes:

> While at school in Dorset I was greatly influenced by Donald Potter, the master responsible for sculpture and pottery, and I spent much time following the firing of the school kiln. It was from him that I learned to respect everyday objects and utensils that had been well made from natural materials - 'craft' as opposed to 'art'.

# Ceramic Stations of the Cross

A special memory of one particular firing was recorded as a poem by Stephen Spicer in 1959. It was the time when Don packed the kiln with a mixture of pupils' work and 'his ongoing commission of relief wall plaques'. These ceramic *Stations of the Cross* were for St. Matthew's Church, Bethnal Green, London. Each relief measures approximately 76(h) x 91.5cms. (2'6 x 3'). One was reproduced in *Christian Symbols Ancient & Modern* (Child and Coles, 1971). Three of the panels are reproduced here [96, 97, 98]

# Memory of a Firing: Stations of the Cross

[96] *Pontius Pilate washing his hands before Christ*

[97] *Christ carrying his Cross*

[98] *Mary at the Cross*

Some Stations of the Cross
at Bethnal Green
the like of which I wonder
if you've seen
were firing in our kiln once
round the clock

Great bursts of flame
from boxwood on the estate
flashed white then disappeared
inside the grate

A day of doubt
then opening brick by brick
what would come out?
always a shock
they had an olive tinge
with hints of brown
if I am right
it was no trick
excitement mounted
as they came to light

Then choir practice started
up above
with angels singing 'Hark'
or 'witness this!'
and when the pieces cooled
their maker blew them all a kiss
with love
to speed them up on high
to some blessed space
and give the crowd within
at Bethnal
Grace

*Stephen Spicer (1959)*

## Metal Workshop at Bryanston

Don's skill in working with metals came from hard-earned experience in World War I munitions factories. While at Bryanston School, Don taught Metalwork alongside Pottery and Sculpture. Outside teaching hours he also encouraged pupils in a number of projects. Besides all of this, he created a considerable number of his own sculptures, some of which were in bronze. *Herons* [99] is a particularly fine sculpture.

Rodney Lawrence found the smells of the Metal Workshop quite unlike other workshops:

> with the forge, the acids….the heat, the fire, twisting of metal. [Don allowed us to] handle things which we'd never been able to before: oxy-acetylene welding and brazing : joining together brass. There was a lot of noise which was quite attractive. For those pupils who enjoyed their first classes in Metalwork, Don would be really supportive; he would show you how to do things, tell you how to improve on them.

The whole Workshop setting was exciting, as Stephen Spicer remembers:

> [There would be] Don and pupil bending over metal, their black shapes outlined brilliantly by the dazzle of oxy-acetylene, which reduced the rest of the shop to gloom by comparison. Then Don would emerge pallid from the Metal workshop, looking like a

# Metalwork and Design

[99] *Herons*, height 36cm (18")

hardened professional, as if daylight was a stranger and the monster he was working on had to be subdued; this might turn out to be a superb crossbow or a pair of gates. Always arriving in the Dining Hall with blackened hands, he had to argue hard to convince those in authority that they were clean.

The Metal Workshop had a very basic selection of tools, as Antony Penrose writes:

[They were] mostly broken and worn out. New sharp hacksaw blades and files were expensive, we were told, so you got every last bit out of them, and then you forged the old files into chisels for the Sculptorium. If a drill was blunt you learned to sharpen it - not with a jig, but free hand, licking it against the grindstone with a well co-ordinated movement. "There are six different angles on a drill point" Don would say, "three to a side and you sharpen by grinding two of them with one movement - like this. You have to keep them in equal pairs - hold your elbow tight to your side and stand stock still - that's your jig". Sparks trailed as he licked the drill confidently across the stone. A perfect result as always. It was a trick worth knowing.'

Peter Glover was one of Don's first metalwork pupils who went on to establish a successful engineering company. He says that:

When I first went to Bryanston, the prospect of doing metalwork was a great attraction. My interest was fostered and encouraged through meeting Don. His friendly, positive and non-critical approach to everything was an invaluable help to teenage boys at boarding school trying to explore and discover life's meaning.

At that time we had a forge, some hand tools, two worn out belt driven lathes and very little metal which could be used because of the war. The metalwork shop was set to work to build two much needed pottery wheels; we made parts for a wood fired kiln and we made and repaired the metalwork on all the Rowing Club's boats. Behind all this 'spare time' school activity lay the quiet unassuming influence of Don's encouragement to create and explore. I greatly admired this wonderful man with his many skills and talents so modestly held.

The first task Don gave his pupils was to beat out a copper bowl. Ernst Michaelis,[1] who came to England as a young German-Jewish refugee from 1940s Germany, and Lawrence, who came to Bryanston in 1963, although separated by a generation gap of over twenty years, both clearly remember this task. Lawrence states:

I was thrilled that it became something round when you punched it, rather like the making of a first tune on a violin when it sounds like something you recognise. I showed it to Don and he said: 'That's no bloody good, you better go and do it properly now.' This was someone who was taking notice of what you were doing... it was a practical subject and you knew he could do it very well!

A fine example of the use of this copper beating technique is Don's sculpture *Untitled* [100].

Lawrence believes that:

> Don's direct manner was part of his charm. What I really liked about him is that you knew where you were with him there was no messing about. If he thought something was good or you were doing well, or vice versa, he'd say so.
>
> If you wanted to try out an experiment with sculpture, say, weld things which were cast which theoretically shouldn't be done, there was never any problem with that. He'd just say, go ahead, have a go, if it holds - it holds, see what's going to happen......you had your own life...very different from the other ordinary school life.
>
> You started off with set items [such as a toasting fork], no doubt made by countless school boys......They were done in particular designs. Alongside all of this there were a few people who were caught up in what he was teaching and wanted to do it for fun. After a little while I was able to go in at weekends when there were two 6th Form supervisors in charge.... about four or five of us used to spend just about all our waking hours there.

Don appears to have encouraged the kind of projects which adolescent boys could not resist. Lawrence remembers that:

> some made a motorbike, others a hovercraft in the metal workshop. It all seemed, for those days, quite adventurous and practical, in the sort of atmosphere we were in, mid 60s. They took the hovercraft down to the river and it worked. The motorcycle of course we weren't allowed to ride!

At various times Don would bring in metalwork samples to show his pupils. Michaelis still remembers Don displaying a catalogue that Michaelis owned. This catalogue contained designs for modern light fittings which a relative of his (by marriage), had manufactured. The relative had early connections with the Bauhaus Group. Apart from any intrinsic merit of the catalogue, it was a sensitive action, on Don's part, to make a point of such a display. Certainly it

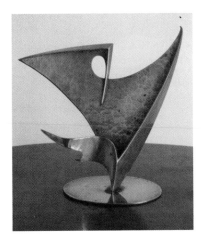

[100] *Untitled* copper sculpture, height 26cm (10")

was an action that Michaelis, who eventually became a chartered mechanical engineer, has always remembered.

Brinsley Tyrrell, now sixty years of age, was suprised to find that after twenty years of sculpture the art of blacksmithing, as taught by Don, had remained embedded in his memory. He writes: 'recently I have been working with a blacksmith creating iron fences…..and will soon be starting on a fencing project of 1/3 of a mile'. For the Hershey Children's Garden at the Cleveland Botanical, Tyrrell designed the *Butterfly* [101], Fly and Mantis Gates. Having developed the patterns, textures and forging techniques Tyrrell handed the work over to Steve Jordan, to do the 'complicated stuff'.[2]

Don has made few sculptures in bronze, the main limitation being the expense of having work cast. In his studio he has a carving of the *Dancers* [102]. Although he would like to see this piece cast, its intricacy would make it an expensive proposition.

[102] *Dancers* Plane wood, height 46cm (18")

# The Archer (1960)

*The Archer* [102], cast in aluminium, was made in 1960. Ian Barker remembers
Don working on it in the Sculptorium:

> The cast had many imperfections that he was patiently filing out
> and at the same time he used a metal chisel to carve the final
> surface of the head and body of the Archer.

The sculpture was a gift from the Old Bryanstonian Association to Thorold
Coade, the retiring Headmaster. At the school there are two *Archers,* one near
the main School entrance, and the other in the Arts Centre. For Coade, the
sculpture was a symbolic work:[3]

> When Blake said, 'Bring me my bow of burning gold', he was I am
> sure thinking of the bow as a symbol of the will........The bow is
> bent simply in order to loose the arrow......the actual

bending….requires strength, determination and concentration……When I think of 'The Arrows of Desire', I think of a boy's whole individuality, the whole sum of his faculties, gifts, talents, imaginative power. None of these qualities mean anything unless they are capable of being directed by the bow which is the will…the function of the will…is to direct attention, sympathy, imagination - the arrows of our desire, which once directed and loosed will find their wingéd way to the mark…'Bring me my spear' must surely stand for the penetrating power and intuition that alone can prove and reveal the truth. 'Bring me my chariot of fire'…surely the chariot of God's purpose in which…we are borne along…towards the same goal towards which He is Himself moving.

# Design

For many pupils Don has had a continuing influence in their lives. Michaelis has written:

> From the point of view of the subjects he taught, and the interest that I had developed as a result, I attended a meeting in the late 1940s of a group called the Registered Designers on the occasion of the 'Britain Can Make It' exhibition at the Victoria & Albert Museum. This was [effectively] an inaugural meeting of the Council of Industrial Design.
>
> In my profession, in a company in which two other Bryanstonians, as well as myself, are Directors, I have specialised in metal forming technology, ranging from the smallest formed metal products used in the medical field to the many parts formed of metal in the motor industry and to the forging of aircraft and marine engine parts. For many years I have been a member of the Committee of the British and International Standards Organisations, responsible for methods of measurement of ductility of metals - and it all started in Don Potter's metalwork shop in Bryanston!

Michaelis also became a Governor at two Special Needs Schools. Such commitment stemmed from memories of the kindness and support he had received from Don when first arriving in England. Michaelis came to the country on the Kindertransport (transport for refugee children who came without parents). The school, appreciating his special circumstances, allocated Don as his tutor, and as Michaelis writes: 'I became the only boy who had Don Potter as his tutor and I owe a lot to him for the help he gave me during those years'.

Another former pupil, who has strongly felt Don's influence in his life is the architect, Richard Burton (a founding Director of Ahrends, Burton and Koralek) [4] He has written:

> Don was a bright light in the cause of Design Quality at Bryanston, and supported our efforts to introduce modern architecture and design in the 80s. While at Bryanston, he gave me the opportunity to develop my three dimensional imagination. He taught us to appreciate the behaviour of materials. Maybe most important for me he was a real artist who expanded my thinking and experience.

Terence Conran, who has become an international name in Design, has written about Bryanston literally leaving its mark on him:

> I can remember all the smells of Bryanston - of the forge where anthracite coke burned and the smell of the wood-fired kiln in the pottery, and the rank smell of the food in the school canteen......

> As a souvenir of my days in the Metalwork Department, I still have the scar on my little finger where I was trying to move an anvil; it rolled over and my finger got caught underneath and was split all along one side. [However, it was from Don that] I learned an appreciation of how art and design fit into society and how important this is in society: the importance of good things around you - things that are well made, well designed, aesthetically pleasing. Don very much lit a flame in my heart.

# The spirit of a craftsman

Don originally accepted the teaching post at Bryanston School on the proviso that he had access to a studio and was allowed time to do his own sculpture. The Headmaster, T.F. Coade, recognising the young sculptor's talent, was quite happy to agree to these conditions. It could be said that Don's terms of employment were similar to those of an artist-in-residence today.

Many years ago Jessel[1] took up such a post in Bryanston's Art Department - this was when Eric Rennick was Head of Art. Jessel remembers that:

> Don was a very shy and private man. Significantly, in my time, there was very little contact between the painting and the sculpture sides of the art department.....It was the era of swinging London and the art world was exploding with ideas which I felt art of all subjects should be responding to…Don didn't see things in the same way…he was a great craftsman in the Gill tradition…the tradition of the anonymous medieval craftsman…. He carried on, with the Beatles and Rolling Stones etc. bursting like giant firework displays unnoticed over his head because he didn't want to see them.

Don might well have chosen not to see much of what was then occurring in the world of art and music. Although always interested in the idea of the abstract, particularly in relation to sculpture, one can imagine him not feeling a great affinity for some of the work then on show at major galleries. Expressionism, Pop Art and Minimalism were not worlds which Don would naturally feel in harmony with. Then in his sixties, he had established an aesthetic benchmark from which he judged not only others' work, but also his own. No doubt he was quite happy for others to tread new pathways but, in spirit, his heart remained with the proven craftsmanship of Gill.

For many years Don was a member of 'The Crafts Centre of Great Britain' which was based at Berkeley Square, London. The objectives of this crafts organisation was the preservation, promotion and improvement of fine craftmanship. The Crafts Centre included several other craft societies under its umbrella, such as the Society of Scribes and Illuminators.

# Stone

# *Athene* an educational arts journal

From early on in his teaching career, Don became interested in the promotion of education through the arts. In 1957 he acted as an Advisor to the ITV School's Programme: 'The Shape of Things'. A decade before that he became involved in *Athene*, an arts education journal, which was launched in the winter of 1946. It was the official publication of the Society for Education through Art [SEA] and Herbert Read was its First President.

One of the main aims of the Society was to be a springboard for debate concerning 'the essential value of the visual arts in education'. In the Society's 'Statement of Aims' (Winter, 1946) strong views were expressed about the role visual arts could play in enriching the 'spirit and emotions of man' and developing 'individual character in the adult'. Research results, they ascertained, had shown the 'potentialities of the visual arts...to reach far 'beyond the educational system to the community as a whole'...and that 'methods found effective in freeing a child's natural instinct for expression of emotion and feeling [might well] prove important and effective in adult experience'.

The SEA was 'convinced that the visual arts are a medium of expression as important as speech and as vivid as life itself... its duty must be to ensure that the rising generation grow up to create beauty about it by its own choice and discrimination'. The 'natural function' of visual arts, it continued, was: 'to put us in touch with the world of nature and with the structure of existence in a sphere of cognisance where neither literature nor the other arts are as effective or appropriate.'

To support these claims the SEA drew on research findings and detailed observations from schools, institutions and art colleges. An impressive array of psychologists, educationalists and art teachers contributed articles to the Journal. Don was on the first committee which dealt with matters of exhibitions, policy and production. Another committee member was Ella McLeod; Head of Weaving at Farnham Art College. Both Don and Mary came to know Ella McLeod well as she gave Mary her first lessons in weaving (see page 72).

The three articles which Don wrote for *Athene* were: 'Studios at Work - Sculpture at a Public School in the South-West' (Vol.3, no.4, 1946); 'The Bryanston Workshop' (Vol. 7 nos.1&2, 1955) and 'Stone and Wood Carving' (Vol 8. no.4, 1957). Other contributors and titles of papers included: 'The Bath Academy of Art': Clifford Ellis; 'Tradition': Henry Hammond; 'Some Thoughts on Teaching Sculpture in Schools': Willi Soukop; and 'Raw Materials for Pottery': Michael Cardew. There was also an article, entitled 'William Blake and Education' by George Wingfield Digby.

In Don's article on 'The Bryanston Workshop' (1955), he wrote:

> Our chief concern is the development of a creative attitude to life - the attitude of an artist… through which, at first unconsciously, and later consciously, the child grows into the conditions and demands of a full human life, lived as a complete human being in relation to the Spirit and his fellow men.

## Pupils' memories of the Sculptorium

In the late Forties, as Gordon Brocklehurst[2] remembers it: 'sculpture was taught in a wooden shed some way beyond the kitchens'. Bryant Fedden,[3] a new pupil in 1942, began sculpting with Don at the age of twelve. He can still vividly recall the Sculptorium at Bryanston:

> As you entered the Sculptorium you went into the cool welcoming scent of stone dust; a mixture of slight damp, of eggy sulphur from limestone and lots of white dust. It is the same in all stone sheds. Yet the Sculptorium was different, for there was D.P. himself slightly cloaked with the smell of stone and always welcoming you with a smile.
>
> D.P. had the remarkable ability to make uncouth youths feel at ease with lumps of stone. Even during the war he always had a good stock of Bath stone, alabaster, and others from which beginners could select, or saw a slab, and straight away begin to realise a dream. Without seeming to teach he urged us to begin to feel the shape, to use the tools aptly, without force or impatience and later to make us realise that a form is as much to do with space as it is to do with mass.

After leaving Bryanston, Fedden went to Cambridge to read History and English but spent most of the time sculpting! Today, he is a highly respected sculptor and glass engraver, who also specialises in cutting letters in stone and wood.

Ian Barker,[4] a 1960's pupil, remembers that Don:

> was always popular due to his ease at being able to converse with (pupils) at their own level, and I suspect it was also due to his rebellious image. He had always kept his hair long but in the Sixties this was also the hairstyle of the Beatles and other pop stars and was therefore a source of much argument and discontent amongst the boys who all had to have their hair cut to a respectable regulation length. In contrast to the other besuited masters he was usually seen wearing his white sculptor's smock and an apron covered with a mixture of brown clay fingerprints and splash marks together with a liberal amount of stone dust.

# Don as Teacher of Sculpture in Stone

In Don's 1946 article for *Athene*, he stated his personal belief that any pupil who wanted to have 'a shot at carving' should be allowed to do so, but after three months it was necessary to do some 'weeding out'. With the need for both 'enthusiasm and tenacity to master the art', there was no 'half-and-half measures about it'.

Don's approach was generally, as Emily Hislop,[5] remembers, 'very hands-off':

> He helped us by pointing out the limitations of our medium for the design and perhaps our ability! [He] would often be working on his own carving alongside us; you could see a lot of Don Potter's influence.

To begin with, Don usually gave a novice either a block of Bath stone or alabaster to carve. Brinsley Tyrrell writes that having been given a piece of alabaster by Don, he 'knew within an hour, that [he] would become a sculptor', …and he did. After Bryanston, Tyrrell studied at the Camberwell School of Art (1959) before emigrating to America, where for twenty years he led the sculpture programme at Kent State University, Ohio. Now retired, he is sculpting full time.

# Tools and materials

Carving stone is a painstaking affair and Don taught his pupils the need for patience. He also taught them, right from the start, how to select their material and use appropriate tools. In his 1957 *Athene* article he described both the type of stone and the tools needed to achieve success. He suggested that the beginner start with some kind of soft stone, avoiding rocks lying about the countryside:

> A largish lump of chalk is a good thing....or some other local stone.....or ask your local stonemason for some of his off cuts.......such as Bath stone. Alabaster, Soft Portland, Clipsham, Ham Hill, Coltswold, Aneaster, Beer, Caen, or anything else he recommends. Having got your material you must find a good solid bench and a place to work where you can make a jolly good mess.

Don then goes on to describe the necessary tools:

> The main cutting tools are: the Point or Punch, the Claw, the Chisel and the Bullnose....all carving can be done with them. They are made in several sizes and as you develop you will find the need for several widths of Claws and Chisels....the Bullnose is used for cutting hollows. The first stage of roughing out is done with the Point, which takes off the large lumps. The next stage is done with the Claw and most of the carving is done with this tool. Chisels are used for the final surface.

> A hammer is also necessary. Stone can be cut only by hitting or tapping the cutting tool. Do not try pushing the tool with your hands, except for very fine work such as eyes etc. Stones of about 9" square and upwards give no trouble when you hit them as their own weight keeps them reasonably firm on the bench: but smaller pieces need to be steadied. A shallow box (say 18" x 18" x 6" high) filled with damp sand; or a sack partly filled with sand, will help to hold the stone securely, if it is partly buried in the sand box or wedged in a fold of the sack.

> A Carborundum stone, Emery wheel or a slab of York stone is needed for sharpening; water should be used with them.

# Alabaster: a pupil's first carving

As regards materials for sculpture, Don suggested that students began with stone rather than wood. Alabaster, in particular, was his first choice for them as 'it is easier than wood, there being no grain to contend with, and not so much skill is required to sharpen the tools'. An alabaster ashtray was often the first carving that pupils did. It gave them a chance to become familiar with their material and tools - claws, points, chisels, and 'two and a half pound hammers'.

However, at the time when Brocklehurst was a novice, alabaster seemed 'the least malleable, and as insusceptible to creative strokes as it was susceptible to irrevocable damage'. However, with Don there to give him a helping hand, he persisted. It was then, he writes:

> I first noticed those hands (of DP) as they began to put some shape into a cold chunk of alabaster......A slow and painstaking shaping of the lump was the essence of the process, and the distance of concept from completion was discouraging to the schoolboy beginner. It was here that the helping hand came, twofold, and this stocky figure, with the long mane of hair, and the quiet smile, chipped away at the alabaster, cupped and cradled it, then chipped again, until I could feel some form as he shaped it just a little. He had made his mark, and I remembered how he taught with those creative hands.

Don was a teacher who would never overtly intrude on the work of a student, but if he sensed that the pupil was struggling he would step in to help. At times he was called on to retrieve difficult situations. Once he remembers having to use all his ingenuity when a 'St. George and the Dragon' cracked in half. The sculpture eventually ended up as an owl!

Alex Wengraf's first carving efforts, however, had a set-back due to very different circumstances:

> I had sketched out a lump of alabaster in a flat form with a Bull's skull motif - I suppose some half remembered shape from antiquity........I was whacking away with chisel and mallet at this poor lump of stone, happily singing and whistling as tuneless and off key as I was wont, when Don finally must have lost patience - he came over and pressed a sixpenny coin into my hand (old money and not quite nothing in those far off days). He said: 'There, there, my good man, please go and sing in the next street!'.

Wengraf did not go on to pursue a career in sculpture but did become a professional art dealer.

# Chosen subjects for carving

As a subject for carving, animals were always popular. Don always dissuaded pupils from attempting the human figure until they had acquired 'more skill and sensibility'. To choose a subject that really interested them was the most important thing, although he once wrote, tanks, cars, planes, revolvers and bombs should be banned! He also once growled: "You're too young for that" when a junior voiced his preference for making a female torso. However, overall, Don's over-riding consideration as far as carving was concerned, was that 'the boy should be enjoying himself'.

Some pupils would make a few preliminary drawings before beginning, while others would sketch a rough clay model. Sometimes the more experienced were encouraged to work with the grain, shape and weight of the block itself to see what ideas might emerge. Even when there was an initial idea, it was, as Barker remembers, 'a difficult process as you always had to imagine the form that you were liberating from the inside of the un-carved block'. The idea of liberating an image was certainly a pre-occupation of many contemporary sculptors. It pre-supposed that there was an image already existent within the block that just needed to be released.

# Ian Barker: Sculptures for Bryanston

Ian Barker, as a sculpture student at Bryanston, had much to live up to. Don knew his father, David Barker, who had been a student at Bryanston in the 1930s and had learned sculpture under Willi Soukop. David had made the plaster wall relief in the entrance to St. Anthony's Chapel in the basement corridor: *Christ carrying the Cross*. While at Bryanston, Ian Barker sculpted three special works. This was in the mid-Sixties and 'under DP's supervision'. The sculptures are still at the School today: *L'Après midi d'un Faune,* Portland Stone [103], the *Gymnasts,* and *Evolution. Evolution* used green Polyfant stone from Cornwall. (It was from this aptly-coloured stone that Don carved garden sculptures of frogs (30-36cm/12-14"). He also carved frogs in Cumberland alabaster).

Having achieved success with alabaster, Don would then suggest his pupils try a different stone. Barker remembers working:

[103] *L'Après midi d'un Faune* (detail), height 123cm (48¹/2"), width 108cm (42¹/2"), Plinth 87cm (h) (34¹/4"), Ian Barker, 1964

on a huge block of Bath stone outside the metal workshop. With a large two-handed saw, myself and another pupil spent several evenings after prep, literally sawing a block off the end of the large, large lump. It was incredible to me that such a hard looking stone could simply be sawn but Bath stone I soon learnt was soft and easier to work with than alabaster.

DP showed me how to pitch into the block, first using a pointed chisel that would knock off large lumps and then using the claw chisel to start carving the finer details before using finer chisels for the finishing stages. It was hard work (not to mention bruised knuckles). I would regularly discuss progress with DP and we would mark out in chalk on the block the next area to be carved.

[In the Sculptorium there was also] a small well-thumbed library …in a glass cabinet that was usually covered in stone dust and wood chips. It was here that DP introduced me to the carvings of Michaelangelo and Donatello. He showed me how Michaelangelo would tackle an arm or a leg in stone. Far from being simple curved shapes they are in fact composed of many contrasting flat or straight areas to oppose the curved ones. This gave the form strength.

# Skills and knowledge for the future

Relatively few of Don's pupils progressed to become full-time sculptors. However, knowledge acquired in the Sculptorium has stood many in good stead. Amongst them are architects Richard Burton and Quinlan Terry. Burton has written:

> He taught us to appreciate the behaviour of materials. Maybe most important for me, he was a real artist who expanded my thinking and experience. He gave me a guide as to where art could be used, which led to my championing the fusion of Arts and Architecture.

Terry's sculpture of *Adam and Eve* (1954) is still situated in the grounds of Bryanston School near the Norman Shaw Building. Terry has spoken of Don's teaching as invaluable: 'he gave me a feeling for stone, how to hit it and to know what it [would] take in terms of detail.' My introduction to architecture came through sculpture and my present architectural work is a continuation of that.[6]

Terry is now a true Classicist who specialises in stone buildings. His work draws upon the Neoclassic style and building techniques of the Eighteenth Century. Since architect for Richmond Riverside (1987) he is presently working on six villas in Regent's Park which have spiralling, fluted, Corinthian columns in Portland stone. He says his ability to 'handle that detail, that intricacy', has come from a first-hand knowledge of the properties of stone. In the Sculptorium, Don gave him the opportunity to work with alabaster, Bath and Portland stone; this gave him a practical grounding which has served him well.

Once, he recalls, he was taken to task by an eminent archaeologist in Oxford who disputed his judgement that the decayed column bases in the Front Quad at Queen's College were in fact Bath stone, and should therefore be replaced in Clipsham. Terry was in no doubt about it from his experience of carving in Bath stone while at Bryanston, but the archaeologist would not be convinced until petro-graphic tests were made in the laboratory which vindicated Terry's judgement.

Time in the Sculptorium has also, on occasions, helped Terry to keep the upper hand. Once, when a mason was doing some fine carvings, he told Terry that the stone was too difficult to carve. In response, Terry was able to take up the hammer and chisel and show him that the carving could be done.

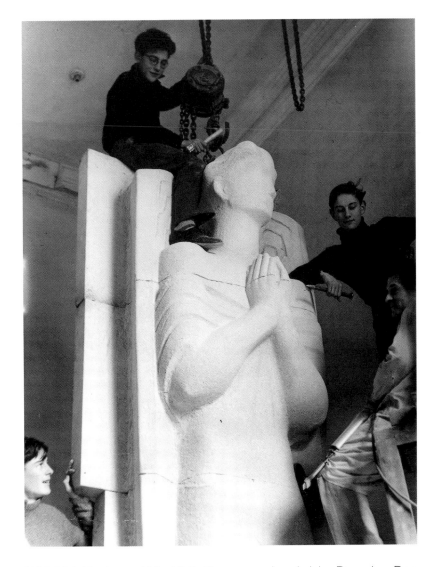

[104] Don working with pupils on *The Angel* for Wolverhampton Crematorium Bryanston pupils (from L to R): Quinlan Terry, Nick Hawkes, Nigel Selby, Don Potter)

With Nick Hawkes and Nigel Selby, Terry remembers helping Don when Don was roughing out *The Angel* [104] in his studio at The Old Stables. Don has said that there were other occasions when such help was not truly useful! However, he believed that by encouraging pupils to 'assist' in professional work….the teacher [was] able to keep his integrity, and the pupils had a chance to take part in work that is for some special object.'[7] As far as Don was concerned, sculpture for a specific site and purpose was in preference to 'the exhibition mentality'.

One of Don's pupils who has followed in this train of thought is Simon Warrack who decided to become a trained stonemason and stone conservator. At the present time Warrack is working on the conservation of the twelfth century statue of *Vishnu* in the West Gate of the Cambodian Temple of Angkor Wat, which he describes as 'a sculptor's dream', being more of a giant sculpture than a building (see page 201). Whenever he is in England, he tries to visit Don and Mary at Bryanston. He remembers, in particular, one visit when Don was 'a mere 86':

> as I approached the house I heard the familiar ring of a chisel on stone. Silhouetted in the window of the workshop was the image of Don with his great mane of hair, crashing away at a huge lump of Portland. We sat down with Mary on the flint terrace and had some of his wine (it helps keep the world at bay), and as he brushed the dust from his face he said, "I say, Simon now that you are working with all these technical chaps, maybe you can tell me, … do you think I ought to wear a dust mask?"

> Mary got in before me: "Darling don't you think it is a bit late now?" He was truly indignant, muttering something about not being so damned pessimistic. He then went on to show me a vast tree trunk which he had just put in his garage to season so that he could carve it later. I looked at him and thought to myself that both he and I knew that a tree that size would need at least ten years to season, and here he was with every intention of carving it when it is ready, and he is 86. The thing was that I had absolutely no doubt in my mind that he would carve it and of course we were both right, he did, and what is more I have no doubt that his attitude has not changed. My dream in life is to have that attitude and even half that creative skill.

[105] *Mary* Purbeck marble, 33cm (13") 1956

# Don Potter: Stone Sculpture Gallery

The Gallery contains just a selection of Don's stone carvings. All measurements are approximate and details are given where available. Don's flint *Tree of Life* [114] is included at the end section of the Gallery. Reproductions of two Baden-Powell figures will be found in Chapter 2. His stone sculptures for Churches appear in Chapter 11.

[106] *Bison* Polyfant Stone length 61cm (24")

[107] *Heraldic Griffins* Portland stone, 76(h) x 91(w)cm (3' x 2'6")

Two Griffins were commissioned by the Croft family for the entrance gates to their home.

[108] *Barlow Children,* Portland stone, height 1.1m (3' 6"), 1965

Don: 'One of my pupils said, "Would you carve my family?". He'd had four daughters and then a son. One of the daughters was rather cross with me because I showed her figure.'

[109] *Christ and his Children,* Portland stone, height 2.4m (8 feet)

The location of this sculpture is presently unknown. It was originally commissioned for East Hackney Parochial School.

[110] Marble Abstract White Marble
height 83cm (2' 9")

This sculpture was carved from a block
of white Marble from the Greek Island of
Poros

[111] *Abstract for Tim Card* Portland stone, height 1.83m (6 feet)

This sculpture was commissioned by Tim Card when he was Vice Provost at
Eton. It was originally situated at the end of a long garden vista at his home,
Stour House, in Blandford. After his death, Card's two sisters donated the
sculpture to the Eton-Dorney Aboretum. The arboretum was originally Tim
Card's idea. Don believes he carved this Abstract from one block of stone.

# The Tree of Life: a flint sculpture

Flints are nodules of silica; extremely hard, but brittle. They are irregularly shaped stones with a whitish rind over their surface. In size they vary from about 8cm to 30cm. Brought to the surface when chalkland is ploughed, they are a menace to modern farm machinery. However, they are an aesthetically beautiful material, as witnessed in Early Saxon and Norman churches and later domestic buildings. In Wiltshire, flints were used with Greensand or limestone to create a chequerboard pattern; the stone providing light squares, and polled flints, dark squares. Polling exposes the inside black of the flint in its broader dimension, as opposed to knapping, which results in narrower, sharp edges. In Dorset, flints were more generally used with cut stone, to create alternating, horizontal banding with stone. In Blandford Forum, and more commonly in Hampshire, this stone was replaced with brick. Quinlan Terry used brick and flint bands with stone quoins for the design of a Dorset house, 'The Hermitage' at Crichel, in the early 1980s.

Stephen Spicer says he:

> was always fascinated by the flints set in the wall by Don's home. Some may have seen a series of films produced by the BBC a few years ago called *White Heat*, about the rise of technology. In one of them, a Frenchman, Jacques Pélégrin, is shown directing blows of different force and direction into a large flint nodule to slowly obtain a spearhead, by knocking from different angles; with diagrams the film described how this forward-thinking capacity of the brain evolved and was already present a very long time ago......Don is known for his work with flints.....and it made me think of him.

At the Old Forge, Don constructed a courtyard outside the kitchen with a polled flint floor. The sitting area is sheltered by a supporting wall of uncut flints which was already there. It was in this little courtyard that Don and Mary were photographed on the day of their Golden Wedding Anniversary [112].

[112] Don and Mary Potter's Golden Wedding Anniversary: Flint courtyard at the Old Forge

Gordon Brocklehurst remembers calling in on Don at The Old Forge, when he was working on *The Tree of Life*. He found:

> Don in his studio working at a towering structure of entwined figures which he had suspended from the roof beams, and surrounded with scaffolding. Moreover, not only was he thus applying his agile, but by no means young figure, to this massive work, but he also was himself knapping the flints....I was reminded of the great churches of East Anglia with their flinted walls made by our medieval craftsmen, and I wondered at this man...

*The Tree of Life* stands about 6.7m (22 feet) in height, and has a total of fifteen hundred flints set into a cement mortar. Each flint had to be individually shaped, those at the corners having to have two shaped sides. The flints for the sculpture, as well as for the Old Forge courtyard, came from local fields. Don made the *Tree of Life* in sections in his studio, before transporting and fitting the whole sculpture together on site [113]. Steel reinforcing strengthens the structure and runs several feet deep into the ground. The sculpture took Don between three and four months to make and is his only sculptural work in flint.

Originally, *The Tree of Life* was intended to overlook a piazza designed by Richard Burton. However, this project never came to fruition and today the

[113] *Tree of Life*, Don working on site, 1988

sculpture stands close to Coade Hall [114]. Brocklehust remembers that: 'When the tall composition was eventually placed where it now stands on display to Bryanstonians and the visiting world, I thought it was very much about the creativity of craftsmanship.'

The mortared curves of the sculpture soften its form while emphasising its three-dimensionality. Openings in the sculpture encapsulate dark foliage from distant trees and architectural features from nearby buildings: these add a further spatial dimension and quality to the sculpture. The silhouette of the *Tree of Life* is strong, drawing the eye up to ever-changing skies and cloud formations. It is truly a striking and dramatic piece at all hours of the day.

[114] *Tree of Life* next to Coade Hall, 1988

## Woodlands of Bryanston School

At Bryanston Don felt lucky to live in 'some three hundred acres of wooded parkland with a wonderful selection of trees: Walnut, Yew, Sycamore, Maple, Plane, Cedar, Beech, Lime, Cherry, Oak, Ash, Holly and Box.'[1] The accessibility to 'fallen trees and large branches' was a joy. In an interview with Byron Rogers, in *The Sunday Telegraph*[2] (1996) Don said: 'After every gale I wake up with a smile on my face. After the hurricane I woke up with a grin'. As recently as 1997, Don promised Russell Polden, a former pupil and later, a CDT teacher, that he would 'remember to look out some pieces of timber' for him during his 'excursions up in the Bryanston woods' [115].

## Three prized sculptures

As a Bryanston pupil, Polden had, at the age of fourteen, won a National Arts competition with his Walnut carving of *Totem Pole Man*. A few years ago, Don wrote to him saying:

> 'Hope you don't mind, but I remember your totem pole/ pondering man and just had to do something similar to capture that impish image.' Polden felt this to be 'the most amazing compliment', and Barbara, his wife, was eventually able to acquire Don's carving 'through some skullduggery with Mary'. Now, at the Polden's home, both carvings sit and 'seem to chat away quite merrily' [116].

On the back of a photograph of Don's carving, Don has written:

> 'Self Portrait! 10" high, Walnut, with apologies to Charles Voysey'.

# Wood and Ivory

[116] *Totem Pole Men:* Don's carving is on the left; Polden's on the right. Polden also made the lamp as a birthday present for Don.

Don has always been more than happy to receive presents of wood for carving. Once a former teaching colleague of his, Clive Carré,[3] before departing for Australia, offered Don the wood of a pear tree he had cut down from an overgrown orchard in Durweston. In return Don agreed to make a small carving of a buffalo. However, the pear tree did not yield the beautiful wood that was expected - in fact it had been rotten inside. 'Nevertheless,' as Carré recounts, 'Don kept his word and when I arrived back from Australia… there was a buffalo waiting for me.' It has been on Carré's desk ever since and is a most treasured possession. Besides carving this animal in wood, Don has also carved it in stone (see page 137) .

Another carving, this time a pair of 'working hands' in semi-relief, are much prized by another former pupil, Gordon Brocklehurst. Having always remembered how Don 'taught with those creative hands' he was delighted to buy *Hands* [117] at the opening of the Don Potter Arts Centre in 1997. He describes 'Potter's *Hands*' as having 'that refinement of form, composition, and technique passed from Master, through pupil, to next Master'. After Bryanston, Brocklehurst went on to university to study surgery. He has written that: 'while privileged to develop many techniques working with living tissue, I retained always the aspiration to craftsmanship, and the endeavour to use my hands well.'

# Bryanston School: wood carving in the Sculptorium

It took two terms for Emily Hislop who won an Art scholarship to Bryanston (1978), to discover Don Potter in the Sculptorium:

> A cross between a mad professor and a jolly old elf hidden away in a dusty, almost subterranean world, [he had] created what seemed like a refuge for artists and the art of carving. The atmosphere inside was informal. Don, in his trademark newspaper hat, was usually humming the *Toreador's Song* from *Carmen* between huffing and puffing away the dust that accumulates when sanding a piece of wood…he showed great patience and taught me to enjoy the process of carving.

For so many pupils, the Sculptorium was a very special place. Polden recalls:

> in that sculptorium I felt a person: a somebody. Don was brilliant in guiding me to shape stone, alabaster and wood. Next to the playing field I spent more time there than anywhere else. Don had that something to make a young person feel confident, to bring them out of themselves and do something worthwhile.

Bath stone or alabaster were the materials from which pupils made their first sculpture. After that, they would be given wood to make a spoon or bowl. Wood came after stone because, in Don's estimation: it was 'tough and resistant'. He regarded it as 'a more difficult medium technically to work', a fact which pupils such as Ian Barker soon came to discover:

[117] *Hands* semi-relief carving

D.P. presented me with a lump of Acacia from which I carved a Centurion's Head. Wood was much more difficult than stone as the grain dictated which direction one could use the chisel.

However, Don also believed that because of wood's 'warm and elastic nature greater liberties [could] be taken with it, parts [could] be more detached without fear of breaking off, and the beauty of the wood [lent] itself to beautiful polished planes and surfaces'.[4]

With chisels and half a dozen gouges of different sizes, plus a wooden mallet, Don would introduce the boys to wood carving. Barker writes that 'the tools were different [from those used with stone]; instead of the point to block out the form roughly, one used large 'U' shaped gouges and gradually used shallower gauges as the details carved became finer. Wood was held in vices and cramps on heavy benches with 'oilstones, slips and strops for sharpening' nearby. The gouges always had to be razor sharp. Don always said the test of a sharp tool was to cut across the grain of a piece of pine, leaving a clear, crisp cut. He ordered his tools from Buck and Ryan, Copeley's, and Tiranti.

Don would always encourage his pupils to let the 'cylindrical form' of each piece of wood influence their design. However, it was often through their own 'bitter experience' that they learned that certain woods would split badly - Oak, Ash, Beech and Box. They also learned that Elm could be carved almost 'wet', as could Walnut, Plane, Holly and Yew. Horse Chestnut and Cedar of Lebanon were two woods Don advised them to avoid.

Don has always been a closet reader, but the boys never saw this more hidden side of him. To them, he was a person always engaged in some physical activity or another, even when he was called on to supervise 'extra work' sessions for 'academically challenged pupils to catch up with their work'. Quin Hollick remembers one of these occasions when Don was supervising. Rather than bringing essays to mark, as other masters did: 'he presided from a chair placed on a large sheet of polythene to catch the chippings . In his lap he was carving a fish on the head of a walking stick.'

[118] *Acrobat* Walnut 21cm diameter (8¹/2")

# Don Potter Sculpture Gallery

Don's major church wood-carvings are listed in Chapter 11. This section of the book focuses on a number of selected smaller works, many of which were carried out as commissions. A number of archive photographs have been reproduced but unfortunately few bear any date, description or title to help identify the work.

Two of Don's earlier wood carvings were the *Acrobat* [118] and *Seated Figure* [119]. *Acrobat* is a circular semi-relief, carved in Walnut, of 21cm (8¹/2") diameter. The female figure holds her ankles as she turns in the air. It was acrobats such as these that Don loved to watch in the circuses of his childhood. This fine, delicate polished carving shows Gill's influence.

*Seated Figure* is different in mood and finish. It is both a strong and emotive carving. Less 'finished', the viewer is aware of the original block - of the weight, dimension and 'character' of the wood with which Don started. He has not let its nature disappear. Unfortunately there are no details of this work. *Seated Figure* was probably carved in the early Forties.[5]

For a period Don kept a sketch book but no longer does so. His usual procedure when beginning a new sculpture is either to make a maquette or to work from:

> an idea partly in my head. As I work, the sculpture develops and new ideas come about. I'm not happy doing a drawing. I can't think in a drawing but in clay, wood or stone my subconscious works.

# Abstract carvings

In the Forties, Don carved his first abstracts. 'It was fashionable', as Don simply puts it. Abstract carvings presented him with a different challenge to the more figurative work he had been doing with Gill. This was also a time when sculptors such as Moore and Hepworth were winning attention from the art world.

*Mary's Abstract* [120] (1948) was carved for Mary after they had been married for three years. The wood is Yew, which Don says 'has a marvellous surface; it polishes up well. You get it as smooth as you can with a tool; chip, chip, chip, then glass paper.'

[119] *Seated Figure* c 1943

Many of Don's abstract and semi-abstract sculptures have a particularly strong spiritual dimension. They balance on the edge between figuration and abstraction, as with *Head of Judas* [122, 130] and *Night Creatures* [121]. To create such tension between two worlds is not easy. However, for Don, the block can be an inspiration in itself, a lead. With Don, wood is never brutally treated; its inherent qualities of texture and colour, strength and volume are always respected.

[120] *Mary's Abstract*, Yew, height 21.2cm. (8¹/2''), 1948

[122] *Head of Judas*, Yew, height 46cm (18'')

[121] *Night Creatures*, Elm, height 92cm (36'')

With some works of sculpture, Don enters the complete realm of abstraction. It is believed that *Untitled Abstract I* [123] was exhibited at Dorset County Museum in the Seventies (c.1974), along with *Untitled Abstract II* [125]. The latter carving is literally mirrored in a fixed horizontal mirror which forms part of the sculpture.

Alongside such abstracts Don has always continued with some figurative carving, such as *The Birds* [128]. When his daughter was little he carved a fine portrait head of her, he also carved a doll and doll's cradle for her to play with.

[125] *Untitled Abstract II*

[123] *Untitled Abstract I*

[124] Don with chain saw in his studio at The Old Forge, May 2002

In 1964, Don was commissioned by 'The Fox' [126] for an inn sign. This piece of work combines Don's skills both as a letterer and as a sculptor. The name of the inn is written in flamboyant 'Elizabethan' scroll, while above it, a life-size fox, in Mahogany, runs fast and low, nose to tail in the wind. The sign's metal horse-shoe support bracket was also made by Don.

English Walnut has always been a favourite wood of Don's but it is now difficult to obtain. *Horse and Rider* [127], exhibited at Dorset County Museum, is a fine carving made from this wood.

Don also carved a Walnut *Girl with Doves* 36cm (14"). For this sculpture, one dove rests on the head of a girl, while another sits in one of her hands. Another sensitive Walnut carving is of a mother kneeling down protectively placing a cover round her child. For this sculpture the wood symbolically swirls round both of the figures.

Lime is a wood which Don uses for much of his present carving. It was, as he points out, Grinling Gibbon's favourite wood. *The Birds*[6] is carved in Lime with a Yew base.

[126] The Fox Inn at Corscombe, Dorset. with full size carved Mahogany *Fox*, 1964

[127] *Horse and Rider* 400(h) × 550(l)mm (15³/4" × 21⁵/8") Walnut c.1970

[128] *The Birds* 610mm(h) × 580mm(w) (2ft × 22³/4") Lime with Yew base

# The Offering

[129] *The Offering*, English Walnut, height 46cm (18"), 1966

As far as keeping records of exhibitions, Don kept none. We do know that he exhibited at the Royal Academy Summer Exhibitions but we only have one or two documented instances concerning this. One comes from a former Chairman of the Old Bryanstonian Association (OBA), Michael Dickenson. Referring to *The Offering* [129] Dickenson writes:

> At the time when the Coade Hall was under construction, I was Chairman of the OBA. While in London for a meeting of the committee I visited the Royal Academy Summer Exhibition and there I saw a carving by Don Potter *(The Offering)*. At the meeting that evening, I proposed that this carving should be purchased by the OBA for presentation to the School as the OBA's gift. Teddy Potter (then OBA Secretary) was instructed to effect the purchase next morning. He duly went to do so, only to find that it had already been sold. I was asked to ask Don if he would do a similar carving for the OBA to purchase - not something artists are keen to do. However, after lengthy discussion, he agreed to do so. The carving is dated 16.7.66.

Don then did a third carving of *The Offering*, but it turned out not to be at all similar. Mary relates that instead of the people receiving a carving of hands releasing a dove, what they actually received was a pair of hands cradling a baby - and this was for a couple who had no children themselves. Although Don will sometimes do a repeat, none can be said to be identical in the manner of a cast bronze. Instead, each carving is a unique labour of love, skill and originality.

[130] Don in his studio beginning a new sculpture, Spring 2002

# Poetry: a source of inspiration

Metaphysical poetry and mystical philosophy have always been a source of inspiration for Don. He reflects that 'Blake always said such wise things' even if they were not recognised as such in his own day. Blake was certainly 'in the air' during the Fifties. With his bicentenary celebrated in 1957, there came renewed interest in the poet and artist. Blake's *Songs of Innocence and Experience* struck a chord in the hearts of many people, particularly after years of aggression and war. His philosophy greatly influenced many who worked in arts education. It certainly underlay the stated aims of *The Society for Education through Arts* (see page 127).

Apart from Blake, Don also read Walt Whitman. He says a line from one of Whitman's poems, *Set sail my ship*, inspired one sculpture [131, 132]. Indeed, it has inspired more than one version.[7] Both are testaments to Don's skill.

[131] *Set sail my ship* English Walnut, 229mm x 305mm (9" x 12")

[132] Don working on *Set Sail my ship* at The Old Forge

# Laminate sculptures

Apart from carving directly into an existing block, Don has also fabricated his own blocks by laminating layers of marine ply. In his Tree of Life [133] dark and light 'growth' layers symbolise regeneration - both physically and spiritually. To make the sculpture, Don first glued 8-ply pre-cut sheets together to make the rough branched shape of a tree. He then carved and worked it to a smooth finish before finally varnishing it. He originally hoped the sculpture would withstand an outdoor site; however, he is now more sceptical about its resilience to weathering. Later, Don carved a pair of *Herons* (1992) [134], two *Dolphins Sporting on the Wave*, and a long, sinewy *Dragon* with its head turned back towards its looped tail.

[133] *Tree of Life*, height 3.35m (11 ft)
Laminate sculpture, 1980

[134] *Herons* height 127cms. (50")
Laminate sculpture, 1992

*Pisces*, (1.09m length), commissioned by Alan Shrimpton, is also carved from a laminate block. Having seen *Primeval Fish* [135] at the 1964 Royal Academy Exhibition, Shrimpton requested Don to make him a smaller version of the sculpture. The original, *Primeval Fish*, is 1.65 metres in length and was carved out of one piece of Lacewood (a type of Plane), although the 'fins' were added separately.

Two particularly strong works carved in the last ten years are *Fauns* [136], shown at Quarlaston Art Festival, Bryanston in 1992 and *Adam and Eve* [137].

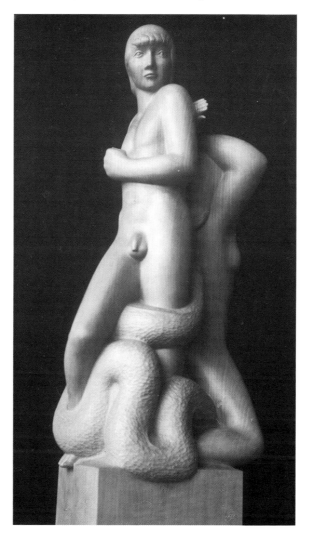

[135] *Primeval Fish*, Lacewood, height 1650mm × 900mm (5'6 × 3')

[136] *Fauns*, Lime, height 51cms. (20") 1992

[137] *Adam and Eve*, Sycamore, height 96.5cms. (38") c.1992

# Harry Dowsett carvings

In the 1970s, Don received a commission from Harry Dowsett; for a series of animal and bird wood-panels. At the present time, all we know about Dowsett is that he was the owner of Brooke Marine Limited, in Heath Road, Lowestoft. We also know he was a Director of several companies associated with the mining of alluvial products such as gravel. Don cannot remember how they met but he does have some photographs of the relief carvings he did. For the lower cupboards of a bookcase Don carved four *Chinese Dragons* [138], while for another piece of furniture, a dresser, he carved various birds and animals, amongst them being *The Loon and Raven* [139 and *The Hawk* [140].

[139] *The Loon and Raven*, semi-relief carving for a dresser

[140] *The Hawk*, semi-relief carving for a dresser

[138] *Chinese Dragon*, one of four, carved on the lower cupboard of a bookcase

# Ivory

It has been a long time since Don carved ivory; the last carving he did was in 1976 and was a piece for Mary. An earlier carving for her was a delicate, interlocking, bracelet; each link being joined to the other and patterned with fine ridges. Once, Mary remembers, a Bryanston boy, under Don's supervision, made his sister an ivory brooch. He took it to a high-class jeweller in London as he wanted a pin put on it. The jewellers looked at it, but then said they were unable to help him as they 'never touched plastic'.

Over the years he remembers carving about twelve pieces; the ivory having been given to him in each instance. Carving ivory, he says, is done in a similar manner to wood. Like wood, it has a grain but 'it is much harder and tougher to work'. Antony Penrose remembers Don once bringing into the Metal Workshop at Bryanston:

> a group of three little creatures like manta rays he was finishing. He clamped a bit of ivory in the lathe and turned six eyes for the creatures. He saw me watching as he filed the ivory in the spinning chuck. "Don't ever let me catch you doing this - it's a bloody dangerous thing to do!"

A finished ivory piece has a very special feel to it. Don always used glass-paper and a coat of furniture polish to finish a piece. The carvings illustrated here [141, 142, 143] show how exquisite carving seems to bring forth a form from within the tusk or tooth itself.

[143] *Madonna.* elephant tusk, height 22cm (8³/4"). The separate hand of the figure is the end of the ivory tusk.

[141] *A Clown* whale tooth, height 19cm (7¹/2"), carved 1976

[142] *Christ's Head* Ivory and Shell

No doubt there are still church commissions completed by Don that have not been documented. However, amongst his earlier carvings are the *Bargeboards* [144, 145] and *Children's Altar* for the Catholic Church of Our Lady of Grace and St. Teresa of Avila in Chingford, Essex. The Church was built in the Gothic Revival style in 1931. They provide an interesting juxtaposition of two worlds as far as Don's work is concerned. On the *Bargeboards* there are the faces of animals (including an ape), birds, and mythical creatures which have an associative link to the totem animals Don carved at Gilwell. At the apex of the *Bargeboards*, portraits of a male and female, both redolent of the work of Eric Gill, look away from each other. Overall, the boards are decorated with grapes from the vine, again a motif used by Gill in margin engravings. The same dual worlds also seem to meet with the human figure and animal carvings of the *Children's Altar*. It appears that Don was then straddling between two aristic worlds…one Gill's and the other of his own making.

# Church Commissions Stone and Wood Sculptures

[144] Detail of *Bargeboards* for Our Lady of Grace and St. Teresa of Avila

[145] *Bargeboards* on the South Porch of Our Lady of Grace and St. Teresa of Avila

# Commissions from Richard Twentyman

Although Don ceased to be one of Gill's pupils and assistants in 1937, he continued to do some commissioned work for Gill until Gill's death in 1940. In 1939, Don also completed his first commission for Richard (Dick) Twentyman (1903-1979), who was a prominent and well respected, Modernist architect. Don's first contact with Dick Twentyman came through Twentyman's brother, Tony. Don has written[1] that:

> Suddenly [Tony] turned up at my cottage in Buckinghamshire when I had just finished [with] Eric Gill, with the news that his brother Dick was building several churches in the Midlands and would I be interested in coping with the architectural sculpture on entrances, facades and interior work. I've always thought since that this is what Jung would have called 'synthesis'. These commissions went on for some years......

Dick Twentyman won the RIBA bronze medal in 1953 for the GKN Research Laboratories at Lanesfield and a Civic Trust Commendation in 1970 for offices in St. John's Square. His first degree had been in Engineering at Cambridge University. He had then enrolled at the Architectural Association School in

London. In 1931 Twentyman qualified as an architect before joining H.E. Lavender in practice in Wolverhampton. World War II then interrupted his architectural work and he went to serve in the Royal Engineers. It was on his return to Wolverhampton, to practice with Geoffrey Percy, that he continued with his church commissions, enlisting Don for architectural sculpture. During the war many churches had suffered damage from bombing or been altogether destroyed. This was a time, when some other sculptors and friends of Don's, such as Mary Spencer Watson, also received post-war commissions for public and church buildings.

In a RIBA Obituary, John Hares (1980) commended Twentyman's work for study:[2]

> by anyone interested in the course of architecture in the last 45 years........his early work [forming] an interesting record of the style of the Modern Movement......By unending attention to every detail he would develop [an initial plan] into a finished building that was always elegant, well-mannered and never dull.

Twentyman not only designed the building but also the interior furniture and lighting. He also commissioned art, sculpture and stained glass from Don, John Piper and others. He himself, was a fine painter of landscapes and townscapes in watercolour and oils [57]. The year before he died he had an exhibition of his work in London.

## St. Martin's Church (1939)

The first commission which Don received from Dick Twentyman was for a figure of St. Martin holding a Cross. This three ton figure in four parts is sited above the main entrance to St. Martin's Church, Parkfields, Wolverhampton. Carved in 1939, it took Don three months to complete and was his first piece of architectural sculpture independent of Eric Gill. The photograph [146] is of Don's sketch model.[3]

## All Saints Church, Darlaston (1952)

Don's second Twentyman commission was for All Saints Church, Walsall Road, Darlaston. Twentyman had designed a new church to replace a Georgian church which had been completely destroyed. Rev. Neil Perkinson[4] says the bomb was meant for GKN but missed. Although it did not hit the church it

[146] St. Martin Sketch Model

Don Potter: An inspiring century

[147] Don carving *The Lamb of God*
All Saints Church, Darlaston

created such a crater that the church simply 'fell into it'. He describes Twentyman's church as having 'a beautiful light'.

Mary Foster[5] was, and still is, an active member of All Saints Church. She remembers Don working *in situ* and indeed there is a video of him carving, copied from a 16mm film made by professional photographer, Len Bailey.[6]

The three works for All Saints are: *The Lamb of God* [147], the *Eagle Lectern* [148] and the *Main Entrance Frieze* [149]. All were carved *in situ*. Mary Foster remembers that at times Don was forced to vacate the building, such as when cranes brought in sections of the roof or put in place the concrete frame windows. He also left occasionally to work on other commissions and to carry out his teaching commitments at Bryanston. However, he completed everything during the years of 1950 and 1951. The Church was consecrated in 1952.

*The Lamb of God* was carved in Portland stone and in height is approximately 760mm (2'6"). The carving was set into the pre-stressed concrete from which the pulpit was made. Having completed the carving Don also replaced the original pulpit's concrete plinth with Portland stone. He also in-filled a spare masonry square in the church wall with a cross and circle. Members of the congregation remember that he quietly carried out these additions with no additional financial requests. His generosity is still remembered.

*The Eagle Lectern* which in height is approximately 1.8 metres (6 feet), was made in three blocks. The eagle, as Rev. Perkinson points out, is often a popular subject for a lectern, coming from the biblical quotation: 'You shall rise up on the wings of an eagle.' Don's carved eagle, slightly more unusually, looks to one side towards the Chancel, rather than straight ahead. Its talons form an integral part of the pedestal. Some parishioners remember Don giving it a hand-waxed finish. Today it still looks exactly the same as when it was first carved; furniture polish never having touched its surface. However, the lectern has had some repairs by a parishioner, as the glue which Don then had available gradually lost its adhesion. Today's repairs are reported to be invisible.

Amongst Rev. Perkinson's parishioners there are still a number who remember Don as someone with a great sense of humour. Indeed, in his figure of Christ for the *Main Entrance Frieze,* again in Portland stone, Christ's right hand is stretched out to the world, while his left hand has two raised fingers in the victory sign. The parishioners believe this was Don's way of saying: Hitler get lost! The figure of Christ wears a seemingly Orthodox head covering which has a similarity to the hat often worn by Eric Gill. Angels surmount either side of the entrance door and there is lettering. In the centre of the frieze are Christ's four principal Evangelists - Matthew, Peter, John and James.

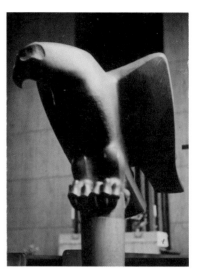

[148] *The Eagle Lectern*, All Saints Church, Darlaston

[149] *Main Entrance Frieze*, All Saints Church, Darlaston

# Wolverhampton Crematorium (1954)

Don completed three carvings for Woverhampton Crematorium in 1954: *The Angel*, *The Phoenix* and *The Three Doves*.

For the *The Angel* Don did much of the stone carving at Bryanston in his studio at the Old Stables [150]. The sculpture is in Portland stone which Don selected from a quarry on the 'Isle of Portland'. The sculpture is 3.65 metres (twelve feet) in height and was finally finished on site at Wolverhampton Crematorium [151]. It is situated on the terrace at the back of the West Chapel, where flowers are placed.

[150] Don roughing out *The Angel* sculpture at The Old Stables

[151] Don working on site at Wolverhampton Crematorium

*The Phoenix* [152] rising from the ashes is both a symbolic and spiritually comforting image. On the back of a contemporary photograph Don noted that his commission fee for the sculpture was £175.

*The Three Doves,* the birds which Noah released from the ark after The Flood, again are symbolic of new life, hope and peace. Carved in wood, they are situated to the right of the altar in the Chapel.

# St Nicholas Church, Radford, Coventry (1954)

The church of St. Nicholas having been hit by a bomb was another war casualty. Twentyman designed a complete replacement for the original church and in 1954 commissioned a relief sculpture from Don of *Saint Nicholas* [153], who, amongst other deeds, saved three boys from being butchered by an inn keeper.

[152] *The Phoenix,* Portland stone, 1954

[153] *St. Nicholas Carving,* 1954

# St. Peter's School Chapel, Compton Park, Wolverhampton (1965)

St. Peter's School was a 1960s Twentyman building. For the School Chapel, in 1965, he commissioned a sculpture from Don: *Risen Christ* [154]. It is carved in Walnut and is approximately 1.5m (five feet) high.

[154] *Risen Christ*, height 1.5metres (five feet) Walnut St. Peter's Collegiate School

## Other Church Commissions

## St Barnabas and St Matthew

For St. Barnabas Church[7] in East London, Don carved *The Four Evangelists* for the outside of the building c.1957 [155]. He also carved a font in Clipsham stone. The cover of the font is Elm, and bears a carving of a baby held aloft in a strong, secure hand.

For St. Matthew's Church, St Matthew's Row, East London, Don created the ceramic series of *The Twelve Stations of the Cross*. The width of each panel is 76(h) × 91.5(w)cm (2'6'' × 3ft), (see pages 116-117). One Station is reproduced as a line drawing (along with two other illustrations of Don's sculpture) in *Christian Symbols*, published in 1971.[8]

[155] *The Four Evangelists*

[156] *Madonna and Child*, height, 1.22m (4 feet) Cherry wood

# Zomba Cathedral, Malawi

The *Sacred Heart Christ* [157] for Zomba Cathedral, Nyasaland (now Malawi), was an Anthony Lewis[9] commission. *The Sacred Heart Christ* was carved from Portland stone and in height is 3.05metres (ten feet.) Don created a gold mosaic heart to set behind the head of Christ. The logistics of crating the sculpture for shipping are still remembered by one or two of his friends.

The English Martyrs Catholic Church at Didcot was built in 1967. Two female parishioners paid for Don's sculptures. Altogether there are three pieces. *Crucifix* which is 1.37metres (4'6'') and carved in Walnut, bears a likeness to *Risen Christ* [154] except Christ's Head is raised towards Heaven. *Madonna and Child* [156] is 1.22metres (four feet) high and carved in Cherry wood. Finally, *The Crown of Thorns* [158], above the altar, is made in resin and fibreglass and has a diameter of 3.05 metres (ten feet). This is Don's only known sculpture in this medium.

[157] *Sacred Heart Christ,* height 3.05m (10 feet)

[158] *The Crown of Thorns,* diameter 3.05 metres (10 feet) Polyester resin and fibreglass

[159] *Crucifix* in St. George's Chapel,
Windsor, Walnut, height 38(h) cms ×
37(w) cms (15"h. × 14¹/2"w.)

Don also received a commission for a crucifix from St. George's Chapel, Windsor in 1970.[10] *The Crucifix* is a small, delicate carved piece said to be in Walnut. It sits on the altar of the Rutland Chantry although it is attached to the Lenten Cross for the Easter procession in St. George's Chapel. Don has signed and dated it: D.P.1970.

# St. Nicholas and Mary Church, Durweston (1991)

Don's most recent commission (1991) was for the Church of St. Nicholas and Mary at Durweston; Durweston being a neighbouring village of Bryanston. Dinah Batterham[11] was involved in helping to raise the necessary funds for two sculptures from Don: *St Nicholas* and *Mary* [160]. These sculptures, both carved in Indiana stone from America, are approximately 1.8 metre (6 feet) in height, and, were made to fill two empty thirteenth century niches in the tower of the Church. In the fund pamphlet Dinah wrote:

> [Don] works with love and prayer…He has lived for fifty years amongst us and has superbly carved several gravestones in Durweston churchyard and other places in his immaculate and freely drawn lettering. He is generous when asked to do commemorative lettering on benches and a number of house-name boards in Durweston and Bryanston. His teaching has inspired so many. It would be difficult to find a better person to carve these sculptures, to fill these empty niches.

[160 ] *Mary*, height 1.8 metre (6 feet), St. Nicholas and Mary at Durweston

# Letter-cutting

When sketching out a slate inscription Don will draw soft, pencilled, guide-lines before drawing the letters freehand. He tends not to categorise his calligraphy although it is generally of a classic Roman type. Forming the inscription he uses a selection of tungsten-tipped chisels of varying widths which he keeps extremely sharp [161].

Letter-cutting is perhaps one of the most transparent of crafts; once a chisel cut is made in blue-black or green slate it leaves behind it an indelible white mark. *The Alphabet* [162], cut by Don, is presently stored in his studio at The Old Forge. Letter cutting is a craft which requires determination, patience and perseverance - qualities which Don possesses in large measure.

It was in his last term at Bryanston School that Quin Hollick remembers Don teaching him how to cut letters:

> "Learn how to cut letters [he said], it will keep you out of the Work House. It will also improve your technique for carving. Before you start you must understand the proportions of the letters." He then drew two lines and quickly sketched in the alphabet explaining the width to height of each letter. He demonstrated on a piece of rough Ballahulish Slate I had found and then watched and guided me as I chipped. His demonstration was so deft and positive he gave me the confidence that technically the job was possible. Having swept the stone dust off, he would often pencil a shape or idea directly onto the bench top.

Lettering

[161] Beginning a slate inscription. The Old Forge, Bryanston.

[162] *Alphabet* slate, height 57 × 32 × 4cm (22$^1$/2 × 12$^5$/8 × $^5$/8")

[163] *Geoffrey Charlton inscription*
Labouchère commission Don Potter

# The Labouchère Commission

Don taught himself lettering in wood while he was at Gilwell. Indeed, while he was at Gilwell he gave Tony Twentyman (1906-1988), the brother of architect Richard Twentyman, his first lessons in carving. Don taught him well. Some years later both Don and Tony became Associates of the Royal Society of British Sculptors. They also worked together on a series of modern sculptures and inscriptions for the gardens of Sir George and Lady Labouchère, of Dudmaston, Quatt. Mary remembers Sir George and his wife having quite opposing views and preferences concerning periods and styles of art. Sir George's inclination was towards the Contemporary, while his wife had a preference for Classic. This led to some interesting debates when decisions had to be made regarding commissions. *The Geoffrey Charlton* [163] inscription was a Labouchère commission.

# Don's first lesson in lettering from Eric Gill

Don did no lettering in stone until he went to Eric Gill. Gill's first lesson in lettering [164] was drawn on two sides of a piece of scrap paper. Holding two pencils together, Gill illustrated 'the cursive origin of the letterforms incised in stone and slate'.[1]

It was Gill, Don acknowledges, who 'polished up' his lettering. Gill himself had originally studied with Edward Johnston in 1899, while also simultaneously enrolling in classes at the Westminster Technical Institute to learn the masonic skills of stone-cutting. In 1906, having acquired considerable expertise, he was invited to write a chapter for Johnston's book; *Writing & Illuminating & Lettering*. Gill's chapter was both instructive and practical. In it he emphasised that: 'Above all things, the chisels must be of the right temper and sharp….sharp enough to cut a piece of paper without tearing it'.[2]

While Don was with him at Pigotts, Gill did little letter-cutting of his own. Instead, his interest in lettering was directed towards typographic print. In 1930 he designed the 'Joanna' typeface, having already produced 'Gill Sans' and 'Perpetua'. The 'Joanna' type was named after his youngest daughter and was intended to be used for fine limited-edition work. This was in contrast to 'Gill Sans', which is probably Gill's best known typeface.[3] At Pigotts, Gill set up his own print shop with his pupil and son-in-law, René Hague.

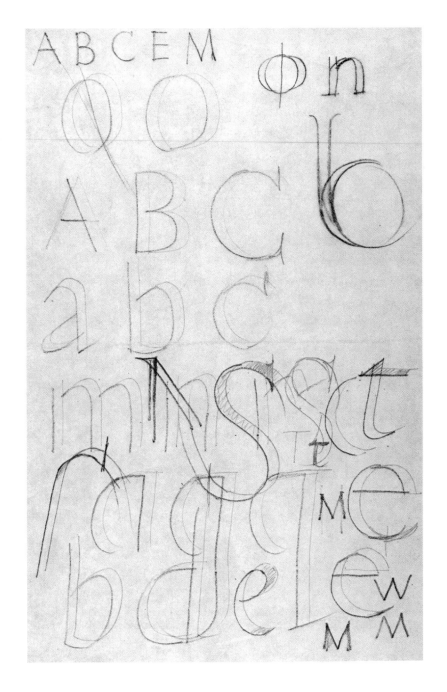

[164] Eric Gill's first lesson in lettering for Don c1931

## Laurie Cribb

In as far as there was letter-cutting at Pigotts most of it was done by Laurie Cribb, whom Gill referred to as 'my noble pupil' and 'too good to live by a long way'.[4] When Laurie Cribb first came to work with Gill, Gill would always draw the letters on the stone for Cribb to cut. However, Don recollects that at Pigotts, it became more commonplace for Cribb to both draw and cut the letters without any supervision or intervention from Gill [165]. The work, however, still left the workshop with the Gill, rather than Cribb, signature.

Don worked with Laurie Cribb on many commissions. No doubt he learned much from observing one of the finest letter-cutters of the age.

## Roman lettering

After Gill's death, in Bryant Fedden's opinion:

> the world of letter cutting became dominated by David Kindersley and perhaps John Skelton (Gill's nephew).....Even the Cribbs....suffered from this domination; it was such that they left the ordinary letter-cutters out of the running, taking all the plaudits themselves.

> As regards Don's standing as a letter-cutter, Fedden judges him to be 'a very competent cutter of fine Roman lettering - better even than David Kindersley or much that his workshop produced'.

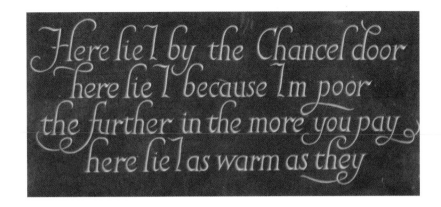

Don's *Here I lie* [166] inscription, which is presently in his studio at The Old Forge, was borrowed from a church tombstone in Kingsbridge, Devon, about forty years ago.

In Brewer's book, *Eric Gill* (1978), the author has surmised that the use of serifs became a convention of stonemasons, as it was neater 'to terminate the letters finely than with acute angled cuts'.[5] The first tap with a chisel, which is strategically important, 'determines the maximum projection of the serif and its position [after which] you cannot alter this point without making it seem whiskery'.[6] The first cut also stops the slate from breaking below, before the next cut is made along the upper side. This second cut, which can be a little more 'determined and vigorous' has a 'fire break' effect, after which the slate is unlikely to burst.[7]

Today, letter-cutters employ a variety of serifs. For Don, producing excellent Roman lettering has been a personal challenge. The quality of his work, in Quinlan Terry's opinion, is even better than Eric Gill's: 'Don is very much his own man, his lettering is bolder, more manly and less sensuous than Gill's. Penrose describes Don's lettering talent as 'enviable', having 'that creamy elegance and perfection that is moving in itself - let alone what import the text might bear'.

## Early Inscriptions

The *Red Corsehill Sandstone* carving [167] with foliage and flowers, is believed to be one of Don's early commissions; completed after he had left Gill and set up his own workshop which was nearby. This workshop was about a mile and a half from Pigotts.

[167] *Red Corsehill Sandstone*, height 175 × 81 × 10cm (5'9 × 2'8 × 4''), 1930s

The *Tapping House* sign, in wood [168], and the *Rabindranath Tagore* inscription, in stone [169], were cut around the same time as the *Sandstone* tombstone, that is between the middle and late thirties. *The Tapping House* commission came from a mutual friend of Don and Mary's. Originally *The Tapping House* was an inn at Great Missenden which was subsequently converted to a café. Its proprietor was the Potter's friend, Phyllis Chalker. Mary says that *The Tapping House* is now a branch of Lloyds Bank!

Don is not sure who commissioned the *Rabindranath Tagore* inscription, but in the early 1900s there was strong interest among artists in the Arts of India. In 1910, William Rothenstein helped form The India Society and was instrumental in introducing Gill to Ananda Coomaraswamy. Coomaraswamy, an Indian philosopher and critic, was an expert in the arts and crafts of India and became something of a cult figure, as also did the Indian poet, Rabindranath Tagore. Gill, in particular, was quite 'intoxicated' by the discovery of the Ajanti Frescoes outside Hyderabad (a series of religious carvings based on the birth stories of Buddha).

[168] Don working on *The Tapping House* sign

[169] Don working on *Rabindranath Tagore*, Portland stone inscription at Speen

Don's *Rabindranath Tagore* inscription is in Portland stone. He painted some of the lettering in a grey-blue colour. Greys, blues and soft yellows were oil colours he often used.

[170] St. Paul's School inscription

IN·THIS·SCHOOL·WHERE·HE·HAD·BEEN·AS·A·BOY
GENERAL·SIR·BERNARD·MONTGOMERY
PLANNED·THE·INVASION·OF·EUROPE·1944·&·IN·THIS
HIS·ROOM·THE·FINAL·TOUCHES·TO·THOSE·PLANS
WERE·GIVEN·IN·THIS·BUILDING·ALSO·WAS·HELD
ON·MAY·15TH·THE·BRIEFING·CONFERENCE·OF·ALL
THE·SENIOR·ALLIED·COMMANDERS·IN·THE
PRESENCE·℗·HIS·MAJESTY·THE·KING·AND·OF
THE·PRIME·MINISTER·THE·RIGHT·HONOURABLE
WINSTON·SPENCER·CHURCHILL
*In war. fury. in defeat. defiance. in victory. magnanimity.*
*in peace. good will.*

# St. Paul's School, London.

Not long after the end of the Second World War, Don received a commission to inscribe an Oak panel designed by Eric Kennington for St. Paul's School, London [170]. It is placed above the fireplace at the western end of the Board Room.

Montgomery unveiled the plaque on Thursday, July 4th, 1946 [171]. Speaking of his return to England to become the Land-Force Commander for the coming invasion, Montgomery said it had been a pleasant surprise to find the H.Q. of 21 Army Group already set up in a building belonging to his old school, since he was 'well acquainted with it'. [8]

[171] St. Paul's School unveiling

# Bryanston Memories and The Roll of Honour

Often, Don would work on one of his commissions alongside his pupils at Bryanston. Richard Batterham remembers he:

> once had a foundation stone to do and he had it down in the Pottery. More usually he would do the work in the Sculptorium. Don would do one or two letters while we were there. He said he got two shillings a letter (in the Fifties). He was probably firing the kiln or something, but when he'd get a few moments he would do a bit more.

As a teacher, Fedden remembers that Don was able to teach the essentials of sculpture and letter-cutting without fuss or lecturing. This:

> was the gift of a very rare teacher. It is no wonder that W.B. Curry, one of the great headmasters of the 1940s and 50s, was reported to have said on his return to Dartington Hall from a visit that the only thing he would like to take from Bryanston was Donald Potter.

Of his pupils, Bryant Fedden, Quin Hollick and many others have been inspired by Don to pursue a career in lettering. Fedden[9] writes that for him:

> By 1961 it was obvious that to sculpt and cut letters was a full time job. So, for the last forty years this is what I have done and blessed D.P. for planting the seed which has provided such a fulfilling way of living.

Don even inspired a teaching colleague, Clive Carré, to do some work of his own, after Carré had introduced him 'to the Biology Department's binocular microscope with built in light. Don was fascinated. He commented how much better he could carve letters in slate with it'.

The *Roll of Honour* (1953) [172] was a commission from Bryanston School to commemorate those Bryanstonians who had given their lives in war. The site chosen was a place just in front of Portman House. In front of this 'very fine writing' stands a sculpture of a male figure 'looking into the distance, towards Blandford' (Alex Wengraf). This figure is the work of Titus Leeser, Don's friend, whom he had first met at Gilwell. Bryanston School

acquired Leeser's sculpture in lieu of one term's school fees for his son. In the immediate post-war era, moving money between the Netherlands and England was often difficult. Leeser named his son after Don and the son boarded with Don and Mary during the time he was at Bryanston School.

## Further Commissions and Memorials

In the Fifties and Sixties, as Fedden has observed: 'the fashion in lettering changed to fine italic lettering and from there to a free cut letter'. Fedden became absorbed in the sculptural qualities of letters…their three dimensionality' but Don, he feels, never felt the urge to follow this road. Instead, he put most of his energy into architectural sculptures. Don did continue to cut inscriptions of an enviable quality. Amongst commissions not yet mentioned, there was the *Alexander Memorial* plaque cut in the late Sixties, and the *Sybil Thorndike Casson* plaque[10] (1882-1976) in the late Seventies. Don also did an inscription in the Crypt of St. Paul's, but it remains unidentified at the time of going to press.

[173] *W.M. Radermacher Memorial*

[174] *John Messenger Tombstone*

Apart from inscriptions further afield, Don also cut innumerable inscriptions in stone and slate for local people and businesses. Around Bryanston School itself there are many examples of his lettering. The W.M. Radermacher Memorial (near the Biology Lab), was commissioned by a father for his Bryanston son who died young.[11] Set on a flint plinth, but made from Portland stone, two life-size, 'spoilt' cats lie intertwined [173]. The linking and folding round of these forms makes this a warm and comforting sculpture. Don has caught the very essence of these feline creatures.

Another memorial which Don carved was for a young boy sadly killed in a road accident in America. For this commission Don had been requested to carve a dragon, but the particular parish church involved would not permit such a carving even when the suggestion was made of putting the dragon's tail round the back. In the end, though, after an appeal to the highest Church Authorities, the dragon was permitted…the boy's name was Prospero.

For many memorial commissions, Don used his skills both as a letterer and sculptor. *The John Messenger Tombstone* [174] stands about four feet high. Carved out of one piece of Portland stone, a Madonna figure stands before an arch with hands lowered and palms facing outwards. A fine-cut inscription underneath reads: To the memory of my darling husband John - Edmund William John Messenger 1911-1966. This was carved when Don was about sixty-five.

# Coventry Airport Commission

Apart from wood, slate is Don's preferred material for lettering. He says that being fine-grained it is good for detail. At one time he used to buy Green Westmorland slate which is formed from compressed volcanic ash. Thus, when he chose a piece he would take into account variations in colour and surface effects. In general, he worked with slate 'of about an inch and a half thickness', using a fine carborundum cloth first to smooth and polish it. Besides buying quarried slate, he also bought pieces of slate, if he could find them, from reclamation yards. At the moment, he has the slate from a billiard table, but says it is really too thin to work with.

Slate was chosen for the Coventry Airport (West Midlands International Airport) commission. The inscription commemorates Pope John Paul II's visit to the Airport in 1982.[12] The slate measures 41(h) x 61(l) cm (16"x 24"). The capital letters are 'V cut' to a depth of about 2mm while the lower-case letters are less deep: as Don says: "the bigger the letter, the deeper". The letters are gilded with gold leaf (an art in itself), the gold also emphasising the importance of the occasion. Above the lettering Don has carved the Papal Coat of Arms with the beehive insignia.

With these public inscriptions, Don achieved a balance between design and layout, letter style and legibility. Conveying the right ambience and tone for any inscription is essential, as is creating an overall rhythm and flow in the whole work. Don seems always to have managed lettering with great fluency and skill, while at the same time not straying from the primary purpose of any inscription which is to convey easily legible information. Thus he has always adhered to the basic rules of letter-cutting as regards inter-word spacing, line spacing, allowances for optical effects and so on.

# Silver Jubilee Stone: Queen Elizabeth II (1952-1977)

When Don has chosen to work with granite he has certainly not taken the easy option, as noted in Chapter 2. He worked with granite for the Baden-Powell sculptures, the stone almost instantly blunting his tools as he worked. For The Scout Association he also carved the *Brownsea Island Commemorative Stone* [20], smoothing and polishing nearly three metres of stone before starting to letter and carve it! Thus, when at the age of seventy-five, Don accepted the Jubilee Commission he was under no illusion as to the work involved. Working with such a mass and volume of stone was physically-demanding work, besides requiring all his creative and technical skills.

Achieving fine, clear, spaced, readable lettering on a ten-foot piece of Dartmoor granite is no mean task. However, Don succeeded with great style and success. The stone he incised was in fact a megalith [175]. It was found lying in a field not far away from its final erection site which is between Ashburton and Holne. It took Don a good week or so to cut the letters. As it rained almost continually, he also had to erect a temporary shelter so that he could continue to work. The image of Don battling with a megalith on rainswept Dartmoor is perhaps not a bad one to end with!

[175] *Silver Jubilee Stone*, Queen Elizabeth II, Dartmoor Granite

As we have seen in this book Don's influence has been felt in many spheres, but his influence on generations of Bryanston pupils has perhaps been the most extensive and direct.

In Bryanston Gallery, a few of those whose life course Don has helped to shape are identified, with an illustration of their own work and some words of reflection on Don.

# Bryanston Gallery

# Richard Batterham

| | |
|---|---|
| 1949-54 | Bryanston School, studied pottery with Don. |
| 1957-58 | Worked at Bernard Leach's pottery, St. Ives. Met his future wife, Dinah, who was also working with Leach. |
| 1959- | Started his own pottery at Durweston, near Blandford. Built a two-chambered wood-kiln in the garden of his house but now uses an oil-fired kiln. His pots are made 'to enrich, rather than adorn life'; they are made for handling and use. He works alone and has up to six firings a year. He never signs his pots. |

Batterham uses a variety of ash glazes; sometimes the ash being nearly all of one type of wood. Today, he is regarded as one of the finest potters in the Leach tradition. His work is represented in many major collections including the V&A section of Modern Potters.

[176] Large Fluted Caddy; iron glaze on bottom, ash glaze on top.
Both on ochre slip. 30.5(h) × 24cm (diameter) (12" × 9¹/2")

# Richard Bawden

1949-54   Bryanston School
Studied at various Art Schools in London including the Royal College of Art. Then taught part-time at Colchester School of Art, City & Guilds School of Art, Goldsmith's College, Hastings School of Art and Braintree College.
Lives with his wife Hattie (a potter) and two cats in Suffolk.
Member: Royal Watercolour Society; Royal Society of Painter-Printmakers; Society of Designer-Craftsmen; Suffolk Group; Twelve Printmakers; and Former Chair of Gainsborough's House Print Workshop in Sudbury.

Richard Bawden is a printmaker, painter and designer. Commissioned work includes: book illustration; editions of prints for Christie's and Editions Alecto; London Transport poster; swimming pool and garden mosaic for a Cambridge house; cast iron cat furniture; decorated pottery; and three life size figures for an engraved glass screen for St. Andrew's Church, Belchamp St. Paul.

[177] *Cardew Bowl*, etching
(edition of 85)

*Don gave me a guide as to where art could be used, which led to my championing the fusion of arts and architecture. An example of this is illustrated by the building which Terence Conran, our client, and I did at Habitat in the 1970s, here photographed by another Bryanstonian, John Donat.*

[178] *Habitat*, Wallingford, Berkshire Area 7,645 m (little 2) 1972-74

# Richard Burton, CBE

1947-51   Bryanston School
1951-56   Studied at the Architectural Association School, Bedford Square.
1961      Set up a partnership with Peter Ahrends and Paul Koralek (ABK) after a prize-winning collaboration (1960 competition for Trinity College, Dublin).

ABK have won numerous awards for design and technical achievement both in the UK and internationally. Their projects are widespread, from the new British Embassy in Moscow to extensions for the Whitworth Gallery in Manchester; from the energy-saving St. Mary's Hospital on the Isle of Wight to the new stations and bridges for the London Docklands Light railway. They have particular regard for responsible, environmental design. In Dorset they have tested and advanced prototype wood houses at Hooke Park. In 1972 they designed warehousing, offices and a showroom on a four acre site for Habitat, complete with children's playground and a play sculpture by Eduardo Paolozzi.

*It was from Don that I learned an appreciation of how art and design fit into society and how important they are in society: the importance of good things around you - things that are well made, aesthetically pleasing. Don very much lit a flame in my heart.*

## Terence Conran

| 1948 | Left Bryanston School having studied pottery with Don |
| 1971-88 | Chairman Habitat |
| 1973-76 | Member of Royal Commission on Environmental Pollution |
| 1976 - | The Conran Shop |
| 1978-81 | and 1986- Council of Royal College of Art |
| 1983 | Knighted |
| 1984 | Hon FRIBA |
| 1981 - | Established Conran Foundation for Design Education and Research |
| 1989 - | Advisory Council for V&A Museum (Trustee 1984-90) |
| 1991 | Commandeur de l'Ordre des Arts et des Lettres (France) |
| 1992 - | Chairman of Governors, Bryanston School |
| 1994 - | Conran Restaurants |

Plus many other awards, chairmanships, directorships etc. First publication was *The House Book* (1974). More recent publications are *Terence Conran on Restaurants* (2000) and *Terence Conran on London* (2000).

[179] *Étagère*, This was part of an exhibition in October of last year called 'Plain Simple and Useful'

# Mike Dodd

| | |
|---|---|
| 1957-61 | Bryanston School, studied pottery with Don |
| 1962-65 | Natural Sciences Tripos (Medicine), Cambridge |
| 1966-67 | Hammersmith School of Art |
| 1968 | First pottery at Edburton, Sussex. Built two-chambered wood and oil fired kiln and made ash glazed stoneware and porcelain. |
| 1971-75 | Second pottery at Whatlington, Battle, Sussex |
| 1975-79 | Third pottery at Townsend, Cornwall. Built a wood-fired Korean climbing kiln and used local clays, granites, wood ashes, irons etc. In 1979 built a similar Korean kiln in the central jungles of Peru, part of the Amuesha Indian Project. |
| 1982-86 | Cumbria College of Art & Design, Carlisle, Head of Studio Pottery |
| 1986-94 | Fourth pottery at Boltongate, Carlisle |
| 1995-99 | Fifth pottery at Chedington, Dorset |
| 1999 | Sixth pottery at Dove Workshops at Butleigh, near Glastonbury Work in many public collections, including V&A Museum; Crafts Council; Bath Study Centre; Cleveland Craft Collection; and Ulster Museum, Belfast. |

Dodd says his pots are made 'because of the heart, in spite of the head'. At the present time he is developing 'textured' pots which have, in David Whiting's words: 'a heightened sensitivity to the properties of clay and glazes [which gives] his pots a sense of regeneration, what Cardew called 'the glow of life' ('Spirit in action' in *Ceramic Review,* May/June 2002).

[180] 15.2cm (6") footed bowl.
Granite/ash glaze over cracked white slip

*To Don, I, among many others, owe a great deal. At the time I did not realise how much. By 1961, it was obvious that to sculpt and cut letters was a full time job. So, for the last forty years this is what I have done and blessed D.P. for planting the seed which has provided such a fulfilling way of living.*

# Bryant Fedden

|       | Started sculpting at the age of twelve at Bryanston |
| 1948  | Left Bryanston |
|       | Read History & English at Cambridge but spent most of the time sculpting |
|       | Taught academic subjects and sculpture in Pakistan and Scotland |
| 1961  | Set up workshop in Winchcombe specialising in cutting letters in stone and wood, sculpting and engraving glass |
| 1981-2 | Glass Artist in residence at Sunderland College of Art |
| 1984-87 | South West Arts Visual Arts & Crafts panel |
| 1990  | Moved to Littledean in the Forest of Dean; set up workshops with Paul Harper, furniture maker; and Matthew Fedden, artist blacksmith. |

Works purchased by many private and public bodies, including the V & A Museum; Sunderland Museum; and UCLA. Library, California. Exhibited at national and international venues. On Crafts Council Index. Commissions include work for the Cathedrals of Bristol, Gloucester, Manchester; Corpus Christie and Balliol College, Oxford; The Parachute Regiment, Arnhem; and The Royal College of Anaesthetists.

[181] Plaque in Stained Ash for Cheltenham Art Gallery, 1989

## Michael Gill

[182] Stoneware vase, height 27cm (13") , matt celedon with copper red design

*My ideal is thinly thrown, high-fired reduced stoneware and impure porcelain with eastern-type high alumina glazes containing phosphorus.*

| | |
|---|---|
| 1941-45 | Bryanston School, studied pottery with Don |
| 1942 | During the summer worked with Bernard Leach at St. Ives |
| 1943 | Exhibited at Heal's School Exhibition |
| 1945-49 | Read Chemistry at Princeton University, USA; simultaneously taught pottery to 'Princeton Group Arts' |
| | Potted at Central Arts School with Dora Billington and designed a twin-firebox wood-burning kiln for Harding-Green. Also worked with Lucie Rie. |
| | Travelled widely, worked in Copenhagen, Helsinki, Israel, South Africa (with Joan Methey), Australia and New Zealand. Potted, built kilns and developed glazes. Exhibited stoneware and porcelain in Johannesburg. |
| 1956 | Leeds University, helped revise Dohnay's Crystal Index |
| 1956-66 | Set up a pottery and craft training centre in Uganda |
| 1966 | Returned to England |
| 1982-84 | Ran the Izlandla pottery for the Transkei Development Corporation |
| 1990 | Retired, but continues to pot and to manage 50 acres of woodland |

Don said to me: Learn how to cut letters, it will keep you out of the workhouse. It also improves your technique for carving.

# Quin Hollick

1967-71    Bryanston
1971-       After exhibiting at Bryanston Arts Festival in 1971 started straight into work.

During my time at Bryanston, Don taught me the rudiments of wood and stone carving, letter-cutting and pottery. I left Bryanston having held an exhibition in the Coade Hall during the Bryanston Arts Festival. I sold all the pots and got commissions for sculpture and lettering. I worked from home near Cambridge executing the commissions I received from the exhibition and then picked up more. Memorials, opening plaques and more recently sundials in slate have been my mainstay. Public commissions include The Ghurka Memorial in Winchester Cathedral; The Oak Reredos in St Dominic's Church Cornwall; The Analemmatic Sundial in Ely Market Square; and Sundials in Girton, New Hall, and Downing Colleges, Cambridge.

[183] *The Sundial* was commissioned as a Christening Gift: the recipient was a Sagittarian (hence the archer). Sagittarians are travellers therefore the sundial must work anywhere in the world. It is an Equatorial Sundial (that is the dial is parallel to the Equator), it can be rocked to the appropriate Latitude. Northern and Southern Latitude markings on the side show the angle to tip the sundial.

Material is Kirkstone Green Slate. Dimension approx 23 x 23 x 23cm. (9" X 9" X 9")

*I have memories of Don in the basement when the old wood fired pottery kiln was fired which was usually accompanied by the odd swear word! I think Don was excited as us when the kiln was opened up to reveal some of the wonderful glazes that he had mixed for us to use on our pots.*

[184] *Donations Box*
Height 91.5cms, (3ft) high 15.2cms (6")
square with a carved cross on the front.

Donations given to my local church were being stolen, so I said that I would make a thief proof box, and so far no one has got into it.

# Michael Kingerlee

1948-52    Bryanston School; was taught pottery and metalwork by Don. Coxed 1st Eight and in his last year was asked to be Boatman to maintain & repair the school boats.
After National Service joined Family Furnishing Company, which he did not enjoy so went into Shipping and got pleasure from equipping and furnishing the Company's new ships.
1966    Married and has 'three practical sons'
1971    Joined Surgical Instrument Manufacturing Company which gave him more leisure time to create four gardens; he has always loved horticulture.
1999    Retired

'Creativity influences my activities more and more. I work mostly with wood, as improvements can always be made to the wooden Sussex barn where I live with my wife. I also make and carve anything required to repair or embellish our local Shipley 12th Century Church.'

*Don showed great patience and taught me to enjoy the process of carving. I feel very privileged to have worked with him; he was an inspiration for me. Some of my fondest memories of Bryanston are from my time spent with him.*

# Emily Lampard

1978-82    Bryanston (Art Scholarship)
1982       Worked with Elizabeth Frink during the summer
           Travelled and studied in Europe and North America
           Worked as a Sculptress until 1989, exhibiting in London, Wales and the West. One prestigious commission was for a presentation sculpture to HRH The Princess of Wales (1988). After a couple of very successful exhibitions in London, and a large insurance cheque for an exhibition which was stolen after the opening night, Lampard emigrated to New Zealand. Here she ran a print studio (woodblock prints and commercial material) and set up a Gallery for local artists in Wellington.
1995       Returned to England, since when she has been a full-time mother. Now with the youngest children (twins) at school, she is 'taking up tools again'.

[185] *Otter,* Cherry wood,
40 × 30 × 25cm (16"× 12" × 10" ), 1989

# Rodney Lawrence

[186] Plate *Samson and Delilah*, width approx. 22cms. (9¹/2")
The 'pottery with people' started when Lawrence was looking at a book of Carolingian, very early Christian, decoration. They are made for enjoyment; the aim is that these pieces 'will raise the spirits'. They are a 'personal shout', demonstrating the fun side of human nature in a world where such feelings often seem buried under what is ugly and upsetting. These pieces possess a positive force of wit and humour and are frequently made to commission.

1963-67   Bryanston School
1968-71   University of East Anglia, read Philosophy
          Worked as a porter at Sotheby's
1974-76   Studied studio pottery at Harrow School of Art.
          Student with Bernard Leach.
1976      Moved to Somerset, built a wood kiln
          Established a studio with Elizabeth Raeburn at Pilltown Chapel, West Pennard. They have three electric kilns and two gas ones. Lawrence makes a range of domestic stoneware, as well as a number of individual and commissioned pieces. He uses clay from the garden for slip-trail work.

Exhibition venues include: Bankside, London; Bluecoat Display Centre, Liverpool; Courcoux and Courcoux, Salisbury; Galerie Besson, London; Hitchcocks', Bath; and Rufford Craft Centre, Nottingham

*Don had a remarkable detachment, he had tough, uncompromising qualities, he was dedicated to what he did.*

# Tim Nicholson

1954-58    Bryanston School

          Trinity College, Dublin; Natural Sciences

1961       Architectural Association School, Bedford Square

He grew up surrounded by artists: his mother, 'EQ', was a textile artist and his father, Kit Nicholson (brother of Ben Nicholson), was an architect. Tim Nicholson started painting in the early 1980s and strives for a deliberate, self imposed primitivism in his work. The process and visual history of a painting is more important to him than the finished work. He has written a biography about his grandfather, William Nicholson. He exhibits at various galleries including Christie's, Michael Parkin, and Town Mill Gallery, Lyme Regis.

[187] *Horses Head,* Acrylic on paper,
19 × 20cm (7¹/2 × 8")

*It is the tradition of Bernard Leach, Richard Batterham and Mike Dodd that I now admire, which I am sure is the result of Don's instruction and enthusiasm for such pots. Although it took me another 30 years to find out how much I enjoy working with clay, I am most grateful to Don for starting me off and instilling in me a love and appreciation for clay and pottery.*

[188] Pale blue bowl, 7(h) x 18(w)cm. (3" x 7"), Stoneware reduction fired to 128°c, with a wood (beech) ash, 'chun-like' nuka glaze.

# Kit Opie

1966    Born
        Taught pottery by Don Potter. Opie's uncle, David Canter (a former pupil of Don's and a founder member of the Craftsmen Potters Association) had recommended Don to Opie.
        Degree in Economics at Sussex University, followed by a career in economic research.

1994    After an evening class, followed by a City & Guilds in Ceramics, became a full-time potter. All Opie's glazes 'are made from wood ash, and include celadons'.

*When I started at Bryanston, D.P. used to reprimand me for trying to carve to a rhythm and whistling at the same time. When I left, D.P. said I should be painting, and the painting master said I should be carving! I have been doing one or the other ever since.*

# Ben Platts-Mills

1962-66  Bryanston School
1967-68  Sculpture course at Kingston-on-Thames
1968-70  Travelled in Southern Europe and Turkey, worked for two years with a stone sculptor in Italy
1970-76  Carved and painted in London, Somerset and then Sussex
1977-87  Painted woodscapes, landscapes, narrative fantasies, portraits; took part in nine exhibitions; built a house for the family
1987-01  Following the 'Great storm of 1987', re-designed the Eye Town Moors Woodlands as a planted and landscaped art work; three large projects on the Moors since then and several smaller projects with volunteers.

During the 1990s has concentrated on 3D work and community workshops in public places, schools and private estates (mostly open-air sites). Current work and interests are the 'Hearts of Oak' sculpture trail in Suffolk, continuing work derived from design workshops; carving crocodiles and snakes for Berg Apton and facilitating the two Bender camps each year in Norfolk.

[189] Oak, height 24 feet, tree carved *in situ*, Highlodge Visitor's Centre, Thetford Forest.

"The sculpture took a 100 days carving"

*Donald Potter, who taught me sculpture and letter-cutting, together with Naum Gabo, for whom I was an assistant, were the greatest influences on my work.*

[190] Sculpture with incised inscription, 1998/1999. Poem by Leo Marks: *The life that I have…the love that I have*. Ham Hill stone 86.5 × 28 × 10cm (34"×11"× 4") and 114.5 × 28 × 10cm (45"× 11"× 4") The piece was made specifically for the Bergh Apton Open-air Sculpture Exhibition (June 1999), and the stone was selected from the Somerset Quarry. It was in support of a large 'waymark' sculpture commission which is now permanently sited at the edge of the village, with magnificent outlook.

# John Richter

1957    Left Bryanston School and went to art schools in Cambridge and Chelsea. This led to learning casting and then precision investment casting. Spent fifteen years in New York and Boston, designing and making prototype models for museums and manufacturers before returning to England to work on canvas and in stone, including memorials.

Married to Margaret, with one son Jed: 'I now live in Wells-next-the-Sea in Norfolk and work from a studio, a converted whelk shed on the harbour. Visitors are welcome.'

## Stephen Spicer

| | |
|---|---|
| 1961 | Left Bryanston School |
| | Studied drawing and painting at East Ham Technical College |
| 1965 | Graduated from Royal College of Art, since when he has been involved in a number of group and community enterprises. One particular interest of his has been in developing large earthenware dishes using watercolour techniques and toned slips. He has also created *Calendar of the Months and Seasons of the Year* series: thirteen framed watercolour and pen and ink studies (diameter 56cm /22"). |
| 1995 | Fletcher Challenge Ceramic Exhibition, New Zealand: exhibited thirty terracotta figurines of children playing. |
| | Spicer exhibits in the Royal Academy Summer shows and has just completed an illustrated story book which is a modern-day fable set in Northern Italy. Now lives on a small-holding with friends and is working on various new projects. |

[191] *'Leeks'*, earthenware dish, 1990s
46cm diameter (18")

*Because of Don I left Bryanston thinking I would become a sculptor, but somehow became an architect. He gave me a feeling for stone, how to hit it and to know what it will take in terms of detail.*

# Quinlan Terry FRIBA

| 1955 | left Bryanston |
| | studied at the Architectural Association School, Bedford Square |
| | Rome Scholar |
| 1962- | Fellow of the Royal Institute of British Architects |
| | Assistant to Raymond Erith |
| 1967 | started private architectural practice: Erith & Terry Architects |

Terry designed the Richmond Riverside Development, Surrey 1984-87. This is a comprehensive development of offices, flats, shops, restaurants, community facilities, riverside gardens etc. At the end of the 1980s he refurbished the State Drawing Rooms of No. 10, Downing Street: The White Drawing Room and the Terracotta Room (restyled as the Green Drawing Room). Terry has carried out numerous other building commissions such as the Maitland Robinson Library for Downing College; Brentwood Cathedral (1989-91); and St. Helen's, Bishopsgate (1994-97). Terry is a committed Christian

'I don't think we can ignore the Modern Movement, but I wouldn't have minded if it hadn't happened. I think the world would be a much nicer place.'

[192] Gothic Villa at Regent's Park 1989-1991. The plan of the villa is based on Andrea Palladio's Villa Saraceno. Terry developed the design to reflect John Nash's preoccupation with the Gothic style.

*Don became a friend and mentor, a symbol that artists could be an important part of a system without compromising any part of their integrity.*

# Brinsley Tyrrell

1955-59   Bryanston School (Scholarship)

1959-64   Camberwell School of Arts and Crafts; the University of London. Married, two children. Worked for The National Theatre

            Emigrated to America, lived in New York for six months and then secured a post at Kent State University, Ohio. Taught there for twenty-seven years, most of the time leading the Sculpture Programme. Won several Sculpture Awards, Research Grants and Arts Council Fellowships from Ohio.

            Took early retirement to have time to complete several large commissions, including *Behind the Brain Plaza* (1999) at Kent State University, which is dedicated to the notion that our mind isn't separate from our body, and that we learn not just through words and texts and books, but through our senses as well (Akron Beacon Journal, Sunday, October 15, 2000).

1999-00   *The River of Life:* a series of cast forms representing different types of blood cells for The Health Technology Building, Lakeland Community College and *Forged Gates for Hershey Children's Garden,* Cleveland Botanical Gardens. At present he is continuing forged work in collaboration with Steve Jordan.

[193] The Gates of Great Americans: two sets of bronze gates 3.66m x 1.83m (12' x 6') for the Bronx, New York, commemorating great ethnic Americans.

*I now teach stone restoration and conservation in all sorts of strange places … I do seem to be able to transfer enthusiasm and enjoyment. This comes directly from what Don started when he first put me in front of a piece of soapstone. So it is definitely his voice that is continuing to will the students to get on with it and stop fooling around. It is also [Don's voice] that tells them there is no substitute for quality and craftsmanship and understanding your materials and tools.*

# Simon Warrack

| | |
|---|---|
| 1972-76 | Bryanston School |
| 1979 | University of Warwick, History Honours |
| 1981 | Helped set up the Guggenheim Gallery in Venice and internship scheme. |
| 1982 | Building Crafts Training School, London (Government training course) |
| 1982-86 | Mason and setter-out/draughtsman at Canterbury Cathedral Attended course at European Centre, San Servolo, Venice, for training in Conservation of Architectural Heritage. Scholarship from 'Venice in Peril' fund. |

Since 1987 Warrick has lived in Italy, outside Rome, and in Cambodia. He and his wife have recently adopted a little girl, Sophea, from Cambodia. Since 1988 he has lectured, translated and published regularly on stone conservation. In 2001 he received an Award from the Smithsonian Computer Scheme. Besides several years work at the Temple of Angkor Wat and the Temple of Preah Ko, Rolous, in Cambodia, Warrack has carried out conservation work at such sites as the Duomo of Orvieto; the Doges' Palace, Venice, and the Villa Medeci, Rome.

[194] 12th century statue of *Vishnu* standing in the West Gate of Angkor Wat in Cambodia. This is one of the most revered images in Cambodia and is now under urgent restoration mainly due to the use of poor materials in previous restorations.

## Chapter One - Early Years 1902-1920

1. Quotation from an article Don wrote for *Saga* no.82/2. *Saga* is the Bryanston School Magazine.
2. *Ibid.*
3. Christopher Wellington, a viola player, is a member of the Rasumovsky String Quartet. He left Bryanston School in 1948. Although he had little contact with Don and Mary during the school years, except for music: 'they have evolved into close friends since'. Wellington's written contribution: 2 June, 2002.

## Chapter Two - The Scouting Years: Gilwell Park 1920-1930

1. W.F.de Bois Maclaren was a district commissioner in Scotland. He wanted to provide a training ground for the officers of the Scouting movement. The Scout Headquarters are now based at Gilwell having moved from London.
2. Byron Rogers 'The sweet sound of a gale' in the *The Sunday Telegraph Arts Review* December 1996.
3. Anne Singleton, née Potter (b 1947), is Don and Mary Potter's daughter. She is married to Barry Singleton QC. They live in London with their three children: Iona, Jude and Kezia.
4. 'My early Memories of Gilwell' Hand-written essay by Don Potter.
5. *Ibid.*
6. Baden-Powell: 'Hiking' *Scout Magazine* November 12th 1921.
7. *Scout Magazine* An article titled: 'World Jamboree' (no date).
8. Newington Article. *East Kent Gazette* (no date).
9. Lord Robert Baden-Powell letter to Don, 5 June 1926.
10. Quotation (1920) from Josh Reynolds, Assistant Camp Chief, in a commemorative book called *The Gilwell Story*, produced for the 50th Anniversary of Baden-Powell's purchase of the House and Estate in 1919.
11. Article written by Don for *Saga* 82/2.
12. Michael Gill (b 1927): written recollections, Spring 2002. Gill has a distinctive knowledge about kiln-building as well as glazes.
13. Quin Hollick (b.1953): written recollections, June 2002.
14. Richard Batterham (b. 1936): interview with author, 31 January 2002.
15. Richard Bawden (1936): written recollections, 28 March, 2002.
16. A.M .Chamberlain (1895-1976), universally known as 'Tiny' (which he was not), amongst scout members, was involved in Scouting all his life. From 1934-46 he was Assistant Camp Chief. During World War II, when the Camp Chief (Col.J.S. Wilson) returned to the Army he remained and continued to run the training courses for Scouters. In 1946, he acquired responsibility for the Training Department at Scout HQ in London. Soon afterwards, Tiny, his wife, Kathleen, and family moved to Surrey. Sally Croome (nee Chamberlain) was then eleven. Sally married John Croome (1956), who was at Bryanston from 1946-51. Although John Croome remembers Don as an 'unmissably colourful character' his own contact with him was limited as he 'regrettably "did" carpentry'.
17. Claude Fisher: 'Rover Scout Personalities: Don Potter' *The Rover World* June, 1936.
18. Lettering reads: This stone commemorates the experimental Camp of 20 boys held on this site. from 1st –9th August, 1907 by Robert Baden-Powell of Gilwell Founder of the Scout and Guide Movements
19. Unidentified newspaper cutting which cited the weight of the

# Notes and Sources

Information received from Paul Moynihan Archivist of The Scout Association, and Pat Styles.

## Chapter Three - The Years with Eric Gill

Most Quotations from Don Potter in this chapter are drawn from *My Time with Eric Gill: a Memoir by Donald Potter*, 1980, Book Edition of 500. Designed and Published by Walter Ritchie.

1. Norbert Lynton *Ben Nicholson*, Phaidon Press, London, 1993. p.46

2. All Mary Spencer Watson quotations are taken from an interview (7 May, 2002) with the author, at her home at Langton Matravers, Dorset.

3. Charles Harrison, *English Art and Modernism 1900-1939*, Allen Lane/Indiana University Press, 1981 p. 209.

4. Martin Gayford, Book Review: June Rose, *Daemons and Angels: A Life of Jacob Epstein*, Constable, 2002 in the Sunday Telegraph, June 23, 2002.

5. *The Graphic*, 14 February, 1920 in Charles Harrison *English Art and Modernism 1900-1939*, Allen Lane/Indiana University Press, 1981, p. 204.

6. *Saga* 1943/2 title of article: 'D.P.' Author unknown.

7. Charles Harrison *ibid.*, p. 159.

8. Walter Ritchie review of Fiona MacCarthy's book: *Eric Gill*, Faber, London 1987. Ritchie's review was titled 'The Book and the Man' , and appeared in Church Building, Summer, 1989, p. 81.

9. Penelope Curtis *Sculpture* 1900-1945, Oxford University Press, 1999, p. 76.

10. William Zorach in Penelope Curtis, *Sculpture* 1900-1945, Oxford University Press, 1999, p. 77.

11. *My Time with Eric Gill: a Memoir by Donald Potter* p.15

12. Walter Ritchie *ibid.*, p. 80

13. *Ibid.* p.80

14. *Ibid.* p.80

15. Robert Speaight *The Life of Eric Gill*, P.K. Kennedy & Sons, New York, 1966, p.199.

16. Author's telephone conversation with Sally Taylor (June 2002). Taylor was a long-term friend of Walter Ritchie. She knew him from the age of seven and he died in her arms. I am very grateful for her help, and permission to reproduce a number of the photographs which first appeared in Don's book: *My Time with Eric Gill: a Memoir by Donald Potter*, 1980.

17. *Walter Ritchie – A Man and his work*, Exhibition catalogue, Art Gallery and Museum, The Royal Pump Rooms, Leamington Spa.

18. Author's telephone conversation with Sally Taylor, June, 2002.

19. Robert Speaight *ibid.*, p.209.

20. *My Time with Eric Gill: a Memoir by Donald Potter*, p.9.

21. The original copy of the poem remains with Don Potter.

22. Elizabeth Taylor *The Sleeping Beauty*, Virago, Reprint 1985.

23. Elizabeth Taylor *The Wedding Group*, Virago, Reprint 1990 (1st edition,1968) Elizabeth Jane Howard's Introduction, p. ix.

24. Fiona MacCarthy *Eric Gill*, Faber and Faber, London, 1989, p.237.

25. Robert Speaight *ibid.*, p.295.

26. Fiona MacCarthy *ibid.*, p.249.

27 Walter Ritchie, Addenda & Postscript in *My Time with Eric Gill: a Memoir by Donald Potter*, p.22.

28. Lucien Myers; 'Donald Potter – an excellent carver' in *Stone Industries* Jan/Feb 1978.

29. Letter, 14 December 1934, from the architect Hubert Worthington to the builders, Benfield & Loxley, concerning the finalising of the accounts for the Bodleian Library Commission. This and further information kindly sent by R.J. Wyatt, Collections Manager at Radcliffe Science Library.

30. Walter Ritchie Review of Fiona MacCarthy's book: *Eric Gill*, Faber, London 1987. Ritchie's Review was titled 'The Book and the Man', and appeared in *Church Building, Summer*, 1989, p.80.

31. Malcolm Yorke *Eric Gill*, Man of Flesh and Spirit, Constable, London, Reprint 1982, p.235.

32. Photography by Claude Fisher (1892-1985). Fisher was employed as the Scout Association's Press and Publicity Officer during the 1920s and 1930s, having also been Honorary Warden of Roland House, a Scout Hostel in East London. He also worked as a Field Commissioner and in organising some of the big scout rallies, camps and jamborees.

33. Walter Ritchie: Addenda & Postscript for *My Time with Eric Gill: a Memoir by Donald Potter*, p.23.

34. *Ibid.* p.24.

35. *Walter Ritchie – A Man and his work*' Exhibition catalogue, Art Gallery and Museum, The Royal Pump Rooms, Leamington Spa

36. Hilary Spurling's Review of *Eric Gill: Man of Flesh and Spirit*,

organising some of the big scout rallies, camps and jamborees.

33. Walter Ritchie: Addenda & Postscript for *My Time with Eric Gill: a Memoir by Donald Potter*, p.23.

34. *Ibid*. p.24.

35. *Walter Ritchie – A Man and his work'* Exhibition catalogue, Art Gallery and Museum, The Royal Pump Rooms, Leamington Spa

36. Hilary Spurling's Review of *Eric Gill: Man of Flesh and Spirit*, Malcolm Yorke, in Observer Sunday, 6 December, 1981.

37. The saying, 'an artist is not a special kind of man, but every man is a special kind of artist' originated with Ananda Coomaraswamy, a Hindu and the son of the Anglophile Sir Mutu Coomaraswamy.

38. The photograph (by permission of Tom Pinion) was taken on his visit to Pigotts in 1940. It was first printed in *My Time with Eric Gill: a Memoir by Donald Potter* 1980.

39. Malcolm Yorke *ibid*., p.236-37.

40. Desmond Macready Chute was descended from the actor, William Charles Macready who owned the Theatre Royal, Bristol, became one of the longest and closest friends of Eric Gill. The villa at San Raffaele was filled with books, music scores, fine art and furniture.

41. Malcolm Yorke *ibid*., p.255.

42. Letter from Pigotts, High Wycombe, (Tel) Naphill 42, dated 23rd July, 1937.

43. Walter Ritchie: Addenda & Postscript for *My Time with Eric Gill: a Memoir by Donald Potter*, p.10.

## Chapter Four - Don's Home at Speen 1931-1940

1. William Anderson, *Cecil Collins: the quest for the great happiness*, Barrie & Jenkins, London, 1988, p.29.

2. This view was expressed by Canon Keith Walker, the Canon Librarian at Winchester Cathedral, when talking about Patrick Reyntiens. Reyntiens made the great West Window at St. Michael and All Saints Church, Basingstoke, as designed by Collins. He also described Collins' tempera-on-board painting, *The Icon of Divine Light*, for the altar frontal at Chichester Cathedral, as a 'numinous and sacred object'.

(William Anderson, *Cecil Collins: the quest for the great happiness*, Barrie & Jenkins, London, 1988, p.137).

3. William Anderson, *Cecil Collins: the quest for the great happiness*, Barrie & Jenkins, London, 1988, p. 47

4. Canon Walker would meet with Collins two or three times a year 'simply to talk'.

5. William Anderson *ibid*., p.146.

6. Adam and the Angel reproduced by kind permission of Canon Walker and the Tate.

7. William Anderson *ibid*., p.42.

8. Author met with Canon Keith Walker at his home in the Cathedral Close at Winchester in April 2002. All quotations from Canon Walker come from this meeting.

9. William Anderson *ibid*., p.41.

10. The sculpture was *Sacred Heart Christ* for Zomba Cathedral, Malawi.

11. The letters are reproduced with the kind permission of Lord Baden-Powell and Rosalind Hague.

12. Thorold Francis Coade (1896-1963) was born in Dublin. He was educated at Harrow and was a contemporary of L.P.Hartley. In 1915 he attended the Royal Military Academy, Sandhurst. In 1916 he was wounded at the Battle of the Somme. He read English at Christ Church, Oxford (1918); and in 1922, married Kathleen Hardy. From 1922 he taught at Harrow and founded the Harrow Conference for Young Schoolmasters (1930). Coade was Headmaster of Bryanston from 1932-59. Information kindly supplied by Alan Shrimpton.

## Chapter Five - Bryanston Years 1941-1982

1. Michael Pitt-Rivers *Dorset: A Shell Guide*, Faber & Faber, London, 1966, 3rd impression, p.53.

2. Ralph Wightman *Portrait of Dorset* Robert Hale, London, Reprint 1974, p.114.

3. Michael Pitt-Rivers *ibid*., p.46

4. There was further construction work to Blandford Bridge in 1812.

5. *Times Educational Supplement*, 12.6.1998. 'My Best Teacher', Sir Terence Conran talking to Pamela Coleman.

6. Article by Don Potter in the *Old Bryanstonian Association* publication, 1982.

7. *Saga* 82/2.

8. Letter to author, 7 March 2002. Anthony Luttrell is an Historian. He left Bryanston in 1951.

9. Alan Shrimpton (b.1937) was at Bryanston between 1950-55, then St John's College, Cambridge (1957-61). Read Natural Sciences and English. Taught at Bryanston between 1964-1992 and was Head of Biology between 1972-80. He was also 1st VIII coach 1974-1984 and has been School Archivist since 1992. Without his help this book would have been a long time in the making!

10. Willi Soukop *Saga* 39/1

11. *Saga* 38/2.

12. *Saga* 36/2.

13. Text to author (11.3.02) from Bryanstonian, Michael Kingerlee, (b.1935).

14. Author's telephone conversation, May 2002, with Tim Nicholson (b.1939)

15. Recollections from Bryanstonian, Mike Dodd (b. 1943) during author's visit to his Pottery at Butleigh, Somerset. (6.2.02).

16. Letter (25.1.02) from Russell Polden to Alan Shrimpton concerning memories of Bryanston School. Polden, a retired Craft, Technology and Design teacher left Bryanston in 1952.

17. Tony Twentyman was born in 1906 in Wolverhampton. Went to Pembroke College, Oxford, but went down before taking his engineering degree to join the family firm of Henry Rogers & Sons Ltd; which he familiarly referred to as *Annie's*. Both Dick and Tony Twentyman lived with their parents at Bilbrook Manor House until 1958. Their mother was a friend of the painter, Frances Hodgkins; with Hodgkins she would go on sketching holidays in the 1920s. This information has been taken from Nick Arber's Introduction to *Anthony Twentyman*, Exhibition Catalogue, Wolverhampton Art Gallery, 1990.

18. *Ibid.* p.8.

19. *Saga* 82/2.

20. This information was given by Alan Shrimpton.

21. Antony Penrose text received June, 2002. Penrose (born 1947, London) was at Bryanston between 1961-64. Afterwards he went to the Royal Agricultural College at Cirencester. He presently divides his time 'between my farm with its 500 dairy cows, and writing and running the Lee Miller Archive, which houses the collected work of my mother, Lee Miller, and my father, Roland Penrose'. www.leemiller.co.uk

22. Felicity Aktas (née Helfer) and her brother Martin, were both pupils at Bryanston School. Martin was a pupil from 1976-79 and Felicity from 1978-81. Felicity supplied information about Mary's weaving classes. Mark Helfer married (20.10.56) Rachel Hickson, who was the daughter of Arthur Hickson, the Head of Oldfeld School through the 1930s. Don's wedding present to Mark and Rachel was 'a lovely oak Roman-letter farm sign' for their converted farm house. Mark Helfer kindly supplied the photograph on page 51.

## Chapter Six - Musical Interludes and Dorset Friends

1. April 27th 1950, and April 4th 1948, letters from Amy Krauss to Joyce Scudamore (Dorset County Museum Archives).

2. George Wingfield Digby wrote widely on the arts. In 1952, John Murray published Digby's: *The Work of The Modern Potter in England*.

3. All quotations in this chapter from Mary Spencer Watson, are taken from an interview (7 May, 2002) with the author at Watson's home at Langton Matravers, Dorset.

4. Val Williams. Obituary: Helen Muspratt, *The Independent* 2.8.2001.

5. 'D.P' (no attributed author) *Saga* 1943/2.

6. Author's telephone conversation with Elizabeth Greenleaves, May 2002. Her sister-in-law was Matron at Bryanston School in 1945.

7. Christopher Wellington, written text to author, 2 June, 2002.

8. Alex Wengraf: written recollections about Don sent to Alan Shrimpton. Wengraf was born in Vienna in 1938. He came to England before he was a year old, and has lived in London ever since. He studied Dental Surgery at Guys Hospital (1961); became a Fellow of the Royal College of Surgeons (1965); did Postgraduate research until his parents died in a car accident. In 1965/6 he took over the family Art Gallery specialising in Old Master Paintings. Between 1975-79 was Managing Director of P & D Colnaghi (at the time the most influential commercial art gallery worldwide). Since 1979 he

has been an independent private art dealer. Published on art related subjects, written regular book reviews, etc..

9. Elizabeth Muntz at work on the head of Theodore Powys. Photograph: Dorset County Museum Archive, Dorchester.

10. Memories written by Anne Singleton in response to author's request, June 2002.

11. Hope Muntz *The Golden Warrior; The Story of Harold and William*, Chatto and Windus, 1947.

12. Marion Whybrow 'Mary Jewels' in *The Innocent Eye*, Sansom & Co., Bristol, 1999, p.94.

13. Peter Tregurtha is the son of Cordelia Dobson, sister of Mary Jewels. Now aged 82, he is a retired engineer and lives in Plymouth. Quotation comes from a letter to the author, 8 July, 2000.

14. Marion Whybrow 'Mary Jewels' in *The Innocent Eye* Sansom & Co., Bristol, 1999, p.106.

15. Peter Tregurtha: telephone conversation with author, June 2002.

16. Twentyman, Percy and Partners, Chartered Architects, 89 Tettenhall Road, Wolverhampton, Information given to author by George Sidebotham ARIBA concerning Richard (Dick) Twentyman.

17. Myfanwy Evans *Frances Hodgkins*, Penguin Modern Painters, series edited by Sir Kenneth Clarke, The Baynard Press, London, 1948, pp.15-16.

18. Ian Buchanan and Michael Dunn *Frances Hodgkins*, Thames & Hudson, 1995, p.152.

19. Retrospective Exhibition: *Don Potter: An Inspiring Century*, Dorset County Museum, Dorchester, 20th September – 2nd November, 2002.

20. Frances Partridge *Ups and downs, Diaries 1972-1975*, Weidenfeld & Nicholson, London, 2001

21. Letter from Mary Fedden to author, 22 January 2001.

22. Mel Gooding *Mary Fedden*, Scholar Press, 1995. p13.

23. Text from Julian Potter to author (5.6.02)

## Chapter Seven - Pottery

1. *Saga* 1943/2.

2. Amy Krauss photographs reproduced with the kind permission of Mary Spencer Watson.

3. Ron Wheeler *Winchcombe Pottery: the Cardew-Finch Tradition*, White Cockade Publishing, Oxford, 1998. p.38.

4. Michael Cardew chapter in Elisabeth Cameron and Phillipa Lewis, *Potters on Pottery* Evans Brothers Ltd., London, 1976. pp 47-53.

5. Bernard Leach *A Potter's Book* Faber & Faber, London Reprint January *mcmxlviii* Definition: Oriental climbing chimney : The bank, or climbing kiln, originated in the Far East. It is now called a semi-continuous down-draught kiln. p. 184-87.

6. *Bernard Leach: a potter's work* Evelyn, Adams & Mackay, London, 1967, p.22.

7. Michael Cardew in E. Cameron and P. Lewis, *Potters on Pottery* Evans Brothers Ltd., London, 1976. pp 47-53.

8. Ron Wheeler *ibid.*, p.46.

9. Letter (15.01.02) from Ray Finch (b. 1914) to author.

10. Ron Wheeler *ibid.*, p.51.

11. David Whiting in Ron Wheeler *Winchcombe Pottery: the Cardew-Finch Tradition*, White Cockade Publishing, Oxford, 1998. p.16.

12. Bernard Leach's Foreword in *Michael Cardew Pioneer Pottery*, Longman, 1973, New Impression.

13. Kit Opie (b. 1956) was taught pottery by Don in 1970 at Bryanston School.

14. Stephen Spicer (b.1943) was taught pottery by Don. He left Bryanston in 1961.

15. Simon Warrack (b.1958) was at Bryanston between 1972-76 and now spends his time between Italy and Cambodia.

16. From 1921, the Rural Industries Bureau was a national advisory service for small industries and workshops. It helped traditional crafts people to modernise their skills (smiths, boat builders etc) while at the same time lent support to maintaining traditional hand skills and methods.

17. Peter Glover was at Bryanston between 1942-45. With his interest fostered by Don, he went on to found his own precision engineering firm *Longfield* in 1965, creating and exploring new and ingenious ways of producing to customer requirements. He has written: 'Over the years I have come

to realise that Don has a rare and sacred quality: he integrates what he thinks, what he says and what he does. It makes him a whole person, full of love' (10.6.02).

18. Philip Trevelyan left Bryanston in 1961 and after attending a painting course at Newcastle, studied Film-making at the Royal College of Art. At the present time he has a farm in North Yorkshire. His father, Julian Trevelyan, was a painter, and his mother, Ursula Mommens, a potter. Mommens is still making and exhibiting her work today.

19. *Times Educational Supplement* 12.6.98: 'My Best Teacher', Sir Terence Conran talking to Pamela Coleman.

20. Michael Cardew 'Raw Materials for Pottery' in *Athene*, The Society for Education through Art. Vol. 7. nos. 1 & 2, p.19.

21. *Times Educational Supplement* 12.6.98: 'My Best Teacher', Sir Terence Conran talking to Pamela Coleman.

22. Paul Rice & Christopher Gowing *British Studio Ceramics in the 20th Century*, Barrie & Jenkins, London, 1989, p. 56.

23. Letter from William Rothenstein: dated 3.7.34. and sent from 13, Airlie Gardens, W.8. (Tel) Park 3008. He writes: 'how one's friends go at this time of life' and then refers to the death of 'our friend, yr sister. She was yr last surviving sister, was she not?'. Rothenstein then writes about Don coming to see him, but Don cannot remember the occasion. The letter is now in Don's possession.

24. Phil Rogers *Ash Glazes* A&C Black, London, 1991, p.85.

25. Muriel Rose *Artist-Potters in England*, Faber & Faber, London, mcmlv p. 19.

26. Paul Rice & Christopher Gowing, *ibid.*, p. 56.

27. Phil Rogers *Ash Glazes*, A&C Black, London 1991 p.85.

28. Paul Rice & Christopher Gowing, *ibid.*, p. 61.

29. David Whiting, 'Spirit in action' profile of Mike Dodd in *Ceramic Review*, Number 195, May/June 2002. pp.38-41.

30. Ben Plats-Mills (b.1948) was at Bryanston between 1962-66.

31. Peter Barlow was at Bryanston between 1944-49. A young potter of considerably talent, he became a valuer at Sotheby's and was a connoisseur of both porcelaine and pottery. Kenane, his wife, said that Peter 'shared some of the happiest moments of his life with the Potters - they were his sanity'. He commissioned *The Barlow Children*, a carving of much tenderness and a capacity to show each child in his/her own light.

32. *Times Educational Supplement*, (8.11.1947) Review by Harry Trethowan. Don exhibited sculptures and pottery made by Bryanston pupils at Heals in Tottenham Court Road, both in 1947 and 1953. Michael Gill remembers being among the first pupils to exhibit pots there.

33. Rodney Lawrence (b.1950) left Bryanston in 1967.

34. Andrew Lanyon took several photographs of Ladi Kwali. Lanyon left Bryanston in 1965 having developed a keen interest in photography. Today he is based at The Book Gallery, St. Ives, Cornwall, and produces both films and books. His first film won the Golden Torque Award at the International Film Festival. In 2001 he wrote *Saint Ives: the paintings of Peter Lanyon.*

35. Mary Potter remembers that at one point, Ladi Kwali wore her best skirt which had on it a print of Queen Elizabeth II and Prince Philip.

36. John Richter (b.1940) left Bryanston in 1957.

37. Raymond Wyatt left Bryanston in 1956. he has written to author (22.6.02). 'Now retired from an advertising and marketing career with Beechams, I am able to sculpt in my shed at Durweston and strive for the satisfaction and joy of getting it right in wood and stone.'

38. David Canter was first Honorary Secretary of the Craftsmen Potters Association and set up the Craft Potter Shop in Marshall Street, London.

39. Mark Littlewood, who donated the Yemeni Pottery Collection to the British Museum, was at Bryanston between 1943-48.

40. Review by Harriet Mark in *Ceramic Review*, 1994, of: Sarah Posey, *Yemeni Pottery*, British Museum Press, 1994.

## Chapter Eight - Metalwork and Design

1. Letter from Ernst Michaelis to author (11 March 2002) in which he writes of how Don 'very clearly influenced many phases of my life' and to whom 'I owe a unique debt of gratitude'.

2. *Record-Courier:* 'Imaginations flower behind garden gates', Saturday, July 22, 2001. Steve Jordan, who works at Steinert Industries, Kent, USA (and who has the backing of John Steinart) majored in metalsmithing and jewellery before gaining an MA Fine Art from Southern Illinois University at Carbondale.

3. T.F. Coade *The Burning Bow,* Allen & Unwin, 1966, pp.111-113.

4. Richard Burton (b.1933) is a founding director of the architectural practice Ahrends, Burton and Koralek which has now been established for over forty years. There is a second office in Dublin.

## Chapter Nine - Stone

1. Jeremy Jessel letter to author (24.04.02). Jessel is a painter and has also done work in radio and television.

2. Gordon Brocklehurst (1932) was at Bryanston between 1946-50. He was then at Christ's College, Cambridge (1950-53), and Guy's Hospital Medical School (1953-56). Rising through a series of hospital appointments he became a consultant neurosurgeon (now retired). He has published over thirty academic papers and two books. In 1992 he was awarded the Hunterian Professorship, Royal College of Surgeons for 'The Laser in Neurosurgery'. Potter's *Hands* can be found at www.badgerwood.co.uk/potter

3. Bryant Fedden (b.1930) started sculpting with Don at the age of twelve. Sculpture, letter-cutting and glass engraving constitute his main activities.

4. After Bryanston (1960-65), Ian Barker did a 'Foundation Course at Leeds College of Art ( 1965-66) where stone and wood carving were regarded as 'old hat'. Whilst studying Psychology at Durham University he organised the Durham Surrealist Festival with Andrew Lanyon (1968). He then began a career as an 'exhibition creator' and from 1971 has organised many prestigious exhibitions both here and abroad, including *Aspects of British Art Today,* Japan (1982); Anthony Caro's *Last Judgement* at the Venice Biennale (1999); and retrospective shows of Anthony Green, Anthony Caro and David Nash in Japan and Europe. Currently he is Director of Contemporary Art at Annely Juda Fine Art, London. He intends to return to sculpting some day!

5. Emily Hislop (née Lampard b.1954) won an Art scholarship to Bryanston. She was at the School between 1978-82. After her last term she worked during the summer with Dame Elisabeth Frink.

6. Quinlan Terry (b.1937) left Bryanston in 1955. He became a Fellow of the Royal Institute of British Architects in 1962 and

has been in private architectural practice since1967.

7. Donald Potter 'The Bryanston Workshop' in *Athene,* Vol. 7. nos.1& 2. p.17.

8. Croft Castle, near Leominster in Herefordshire, is now a National Trust property.

## Chapter Ten - Wood and Ivory

1. *Athene,* Vol. 3, 1946.

2. Byron Rogers Arts Review: 'The sweet sound of a gale' *Sunday Telegraph,* 22 December, 1996.

3. Dr. Clive Carré taught Biology at Bryanston with Dick Harthan between 1960-64: 'In my 'spare' time, late evenings, after most of the boys were in bed, I worked in the woodwork shop, which was adjacent to where Don would also be working. On odd occasions we chatted about his work, and about the sculptures of some of his pupils. I have vivid memories of his enthusiasm and the modest way in which he told me about his various sculptures.'

4. *Athene,* Vol. 8. Autumn 1957, p.22.

5. *Seated Figure* is illustrated in *Saga* 1943/2 in 'D.P. article. Photographer is given as A.P. Davies.

6. *The Birds*: photography by Bill Carpenter-Jacobs [BC-J] (1914-1990). BC-J taught at Bryanston between 1942-1975 and was Head of English. His son, Rupert Carpenter-Jacobs, has written (18.06.02) :'he was a lifetime photographer who was never satisfied with his standards! He developed and printed all his b/w pictures and latterly some of his colour ones. The Potter and C-J children were all the same age/great friends. Don's cello playing was a bonus. My father taught bassoon and my mother, Margaret, flute.'

7. The author has a second sculpture of *Set Sail My Ship,* 2001.

## Chapter Eleven - Church Commissions, Stone and Wood Sculptures

1. Don Potter *Memoires* in exhibition catalogue: *Anthony Twentyman,* Wolverhampton Art Gallery & Museum, 1990, p.12.

2. John Hares Obituary: Journal of the *Royal Institute of British Architects,* 1980..

3. Recently discovered Don's stone maquette for St Martin's

Church, Wolverhampton. Photography Richard Toll.

4.  I am indebted to Rev. Neil Perkinson for much valuable information.

5.  Mary Foster, now aged 82 years, is a Church Warden of All Saints Church, Darlaston and remembers Don working at the Church.

6.  Len Bailey, now deceased, was a professional photographer in the Church congregation. In 1972 he made video copies from the original film. Some members of the congregation still have copies. Bailey's copyright now remains with All Saints Church.

7.  St. Barnabas Church, Grove Road, London E3 5TG

8.  Heather Child & Dorothy Colles, *Christian Symbols: ancient and modern*, G. Bell & Sons Ltd., 1971.

9.  Don received several London commissions from the architect, Anthony Lewis. Mary Potter recalls Lewis was born in Cumberland, educated at Weymouth College and Bournemouth Art School. He provided the illustrations to a book about London church architecture: Mary Crawford, *Who is this?* Faith Press, Westminster, 1959.

10.  Reproduced by kind permission of the Dean and Canons of Windsor St. George's Chapel, Windsor.

11.  Dinah Batterham, wife of Richard Batterham and parishioner of St.Nicholas and Mary Church, Durweston.


## Chapter Twelve - Lettering

1.  Photograph (Plate no.4) reproduced from *My Time with Eric Gill: a Memoir by Donald Potter.*

2.  Fiona MacCarthy *Eric Gill*, Faber and Faber, London, 1989, p.45.

3.  Roy Brewer *Eric Gill: the man who loved letters*, Frederick Muller Ltd., 1973, p. 51.

4.  Fiona MacCarthy *ibid.*, p.199.

5.  Roy Brewer *ibid.*, p. 20.

6.  David Kindersley & Lida Lopes Cardozo, *Letters Slate Cut*, Cardozo Kindersley Editions, Cambridge 1990 p.30.

7.  *Ibid.* p.30.

8.  The Pauline Apposition, 1946, p.50. Information kindly sent by School Archivist, Simon May.

9.  Letter to author from Bryant Fedden, 21.04.02.

10.  St. Paul's Church, Convent Garden. The inscription reads:

In loving remembrance of Sybil Thorndike Casson CH. DBE . LLD. D.Litt Actress and Musician Born October 24th 1882 died June 9th 1976 my head was in the skies and the glory of God was upon me Saint Joan

12.  Bill Rademacher was a pupil at Bryanston between 1962-67. He died in 1989.

13.  To commemorate the visit of His Holiness Pope John Paul 11 to Coventry Airport Whit Sunday May 30th 1982. Thanks to Simon Gray for this information at West Midlands International Airport.


## Photography Credits

I would like to thank all those who have generously given permission for photography and/or photographic reproduction, including:

Rev'd. Neil Perkinson on behalf of the late Len Bailey [147, 149]; Stephen Brayne [188]; Gordon Brocklehurst [117]; Nick Wilcox-Brown [176]; Nick Carter and Quinlan Terry [192]; John Donat [178]; Dorset County Museum Archives [60, 62, 63, 64, 65, 68, 73, 74, 75];Caroline Duah [77, 78]; Rupert Carpenter-Jacobs for his father Bill Carpenter-Jacobs [128]; Chloë Battle [32, 36] with kind permission of the Warden and Scolars of Winchester College.; Claude Fisher (1892-1985) [167, 168, 35]; Mark Helfer [45]; Andrew Lanyon [103, 95]; St. Paul's School [169]; Richard de Peyer [92]; Tom Pinion [37, 164]; Russell Pollden [116]; Don Potter [54]; The Scout Association [6, 8, 9, 12, 13, 15, 16, 17, 22, 23, 24, 25, 26]; Sandra Spencer [136, 137]; Tate Britain and with kind permission of Canon Keith Walker [42]; Walter Ritchie/Sally Taylor [29, 128, 133]; Richard Toll [146, 118]; Dean and Canons of Windsor St. George's Chapel [159].

Every endeavour has been made to trace the source of photographs used in this book; my apologies for any omissions in the acknowledgements where we have not succeeded.

# A

# B

# C

Index

*Primeval Fish* 155

# Q

Queen's College, Oxford 134

# R

Radcliffe Science Library, Oxford 36
Ravilious, Eric 40
Read, Herbert 34,47,127
Red sandstone inscription 175
Reeves, May 34
Rennick, Eric 126
Reynolds, Josh 6,8,27
Reyntiens, Patrick 47
Richter, John 113, 197
Ritchie, Walter 27,30,31,38,39,203
Rodin, Auguste 25.28
Rogers, Byron 9, 144
Rogers, Phil 108
Roll of Honour, Bryanston School 178,179
Rose, Muriel 108
Rothenstein, John 34
Rothenstein, William 28,108,176
Royal Academy Summer Exhibition 152
Royal Society of British Sculptors 56,172
Rubbra, Edmund 46, (Antoinette Rubbra, 46)
Rural Music School, Dorset 75

# S

*Sacred Heart Christ* 167,204
*Saga* Bryanston School Magazine 55,57,78,113,114 etc.
*St. Sebastian*, Winchester College 36,39
Scott, William 76
Scudamore, Joyce 74.95
*Sea Horses*, Morecambe Hotel 41
*Seated Figure* 148

Second Tettenhall Scout Group, see Tony Twentyman
Selby, N. 135
Shrimpton, Alan 56,70,106,155,204
*Silver Jubilee Stone* 181
Singleton, Anne (nee Potter) 61,62-67;79,81-84
Skeaping, John 24
Skelton, John (Gill's nephew) 30,174
Slab Castle 43,46
Society of Education through Art (SEA) 71,127
Soukop, Willi 57,132,
Speaight, Robert 32,34
Speen 46 et seq.
Spencer Watson, Mary 24-27;75-81;85-88;94,160
Spicer, Stephen 100,105,111,114,116-18;140,198
Spurling, Hilary 39
St. Anthony's Chapel. Bryanston 132
St. Barnabas' Church, East London 166
St. George's Chapel, Windsor 168
St. Martin's Church, Wolverhampton 59.161
St. Matthew's Church, London 116,166
St. Nicholas' Church, Coventry 164
St. Nicholas, Durweston 169
St. Paul's School 177
St. Peter's Collegiate School Chapel, Wolverhampton 165
St. Peter's, Gorleston-on-Sea 36,37
*Stations of the Cross* 116
Stirling, John 78
Sturminster Newton 52

# T

*Tagore, Rabindranath* 176, 177
*Take Sail My Ship* 153
*Tapping House* 176
Tate Britain 25
Tate Gallery 90
Taylor, Elizabeth (nee Coles) 33,34
Taylor, Leo 106
Taylor, Sally 31,203
Tegetmeier, Denis 32 Petra Gill, wife of Tegetmeier, 32,35
Terry, Quinlan 134,135,140,175,199

# U

# V

# W

# XYZ

I would like to thank the many people who have given me support in the production of this book. Help has come in a myriad of ways; from finance and sponsorship to 'behind-the-scenes' research done on my behalf. I am truly grateful for the financial support given by Sir Terence Conran, David Wynne-Morgan and Tom Wheare, Headmaster of Bryanston School. My thanks also go to the printers, Brown & Son, for their sponsorship and to members of their staff; in particular Ainslie Chivers and Chris Goodchild. I would also like to offer special thanks to Richard de Peyer at Dorset County Museum, Dorchester; and Paul Moynihan, Archivist of The Scout Association.

Without the written contributions from former staff and pupils of Bryanston School the book would lack much valuable information, so thank-you all! Others I would particularly like to thank are Lord Baden-Powell; Rachel Bairsto, Ditchling Museum; Dinah Batterham; Tim Boon, Alpha House Gallery, Sherborne; Joanna Cave; Cheltenham Art Gallery; Derek Chambers; Darlaston Methodist Church; Greg Colbourn; Enid Davies; James Cook, Vice-Provost of Eton; Sally Croome; City Archivist and Staff at Wolverhampton Archives; Dr. Geoffrey Day, Winchester College; Caroline Duah; Mary Fedden; Ray Finch; Mary Foster; Stephen Gray, West Midlands International Airport; Hackney Archives Department; Malcolm Barr-Hamilton, Tower Hamlets Archivist; Jon Harris; Rosalind Hague; Mark Helfer; Marjorie Hookham; Tom Light; Simon May, Archivist at St. Paul's School, London; Petronella McNaughten; Madeleine Moyne; Rev. Neil Perkinson, All Saints' Church, Darlaston; Barry Singleton; Sally Taylor; Fr. Simon Thomson of English Martyrs Catholic Church, Didcot; George Sidebotham of Twentyman, Percy & Partners, Wolverhampton; Mary Spencer Watson; Pat Styles; Richard Toll; Peter Tregurtha; Canon Keith Walker, Winchester Cathedral; David Whiting; Sara Wilkinson; Joseph Wisdom, Librarian at St. Paul's Cathedral; and Robert Wyatt, Collections Manager at Radcliffe Science Library. Thanks also to David Burnett, Dovecote Press; Priscilla Goodfield; Vicky Isley and Tim Craven at Southampton Art Gallery; Roger Peers; Roger Smith; Kathleen Watkins, Penwith Gallery; Christopher Webster, Tate, London; Marion Whybrow; Faith Widdecombe; the Warden and Scolars of Winchester College; and St. Peter's Collegiate Chapel, Wolverhampton.

To these people and to all others who have helped in any way - thank you!

# Acknowledgements

# Vivienne Light

Vivienne Light was born in Dorset (1947). She is married with three children. Initially trained in music at Dartington College of Arts she taught for several years. After a Masters Degree in Education (Open University) she became involved in research in computer based learning, publishing a number of journal articles. In parallel with this activity she has always maintained an interest in the arts. As well as exhibiting her own mixed media work, she is a founder member of Paperweight (a national group of paper artists) and Chair of 2D3D South Contemporary Art. In 1995 she was elected Fellow of the Royal Society of Arts. In 2000, she established Canterton Books and now works mainly as a freelance writer. Working with designer, Sarah Jane Jackson, *Re-inventing the Landscape: contemporary painters and Dorset* (Canterton Books) was published in 2001.

# Sarah Jane Jackson

Sarah graduated in 1997 from the University of Portsmouth with a BA (Hons) in Art, Design & Media, where she specialised in typographic design. Since graduating, Sarah has worked as a designer in the field of education, firstly for the University of Portsmouth and currently as the Design Co-ordinator at King Alfred's, Winchester. In April 2002 she was part of the team that won a Gold Merit Award from HEIST, the education marketing body, for the 2002 King Alfred's Postgraduate Prospectus.

*Don Potter: an inspiring century* is the second publication that Sarah has designed for Canterton Books - and hopefully not the last!

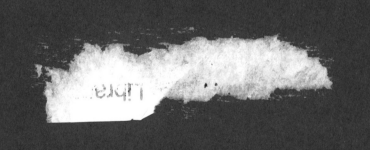